Dedicated with deep gratitude to the many librarians who, through the years, have helped my research and even suggested book ideas, especially Gretchen Bell of the Nanuet Public Library, Nanuet, New York.
—L.P.

To my good friends Andy Day and Peter Brueggeman.
—N.W.

Words appearing in **boldface** type in the main text
are defined in the Glossary.

LIBRARY OF CONGRESS CATALOGING-IN-PUBLICATION DATA
Pringle, Laurence P. Scholastic encyclopedia of animals / by Laurence Pringle ; photographs by Norbert Wu.
p. cm. ∗ 1. Animals—Encyclopedias, Juvenile. [1. Animals—Encyclopedias.] I. Wu, Norbert, ill. II. Title.
QL49 .P78 2001 ∗ 590'.3—dc21 ∗ 00-049660 ∗ ISBN 0-590-52253-1

10 9 8 7 6 5 4 3   03 04 05
Printed in the U.S.A.   23

First printing, August 2001

Photo credits: All photographs by Norbert Wu except for those on the following pages: Page 10 (bottom): Merlin D. Tuttle/Bat Conservation International; page 12: Alan G. Nelson/Dembinsky Photo Associates, Inc.; page 18: © Andy Day/Norbert Wu Productions; page 23: Anup Shah/DPA, Inc.; page 31: © Andy Day/Norbert Wu Productions; page 36: © Andy Day/Norbert Wu Productions; page 43: © Andy Day/ Norbert Wu Productions; page 44: Michel Gunther/Peter Arnold, Inc.; page 49: © Andy Day/Norbert Wu Productions; page 52: © Andrew Fornasier/Norbert Wu Productions; page 55: © Andrew Fornasier/Norbert Wu Productions; page 61: Fritz Polking/DPA, Inc.; page 70: © Andrew Fornasier/Norbert Wu Productions; page 82: © Andrew Fornasier/Norbert Wu Productions; page 84 (bottom): E. R. Degginger/DPA, Inc.; page 85: © Andy Day/Norbert Wu Productions; page 87: Rod Planck/Photo Researchers; page 88: © Andrew Fornasier/Norbert Wu Productions; page 90 and back cover: © Andy Day/Norbert Wu Productions; page 95: Gregory G. Dimijian/Photo Researchers; page 119: © Andy Day/Norbert Wu Productions; page 122: Dan Dempster/DPA, Inc.

SCIENCE CONSULTANT: Nancy Simmons, Department of Mammology,
The American Museum of Natural History
PRONUNCIATION CONSULTANT: John K. Bollard
BOOK DESIGN: Nancy Sabato
COMPOSITION: Brad Walrod

∗ ∗ ∗

Scholastic Encyclopedia of ANIMALS

Laurence Pringle * PHOTOGRAPHS BY Norbert Wu

Table of Contents

Introduction

From an early age, you have probably been curious about family pets, animals at the zoo, and creatures—big or little, wild or tame—that live in your neighborhood. Animals are fascinating!

When you see an animal, one of the first things you want to know is its name. Then other questions arise. Why does the animal behave the way it does? Why is it a certain color? How is it connected to other living things?

Sometimes such questions can lead to a career as a veterinarian, a wildlife biologist, or to another profession that may bring daily work with animals. More often they lead people to remain curious about animals all their lives. Usually, adults who plant flowers for butterflies or who put food out for birds were once children who asked questions about ants, frogs, or alligators.

This book answers some of those questions. Earth, our planet, is home to a rich variety of living things. This variety is called Earth's biodiversity. If Earth had just one kind of environment there wouldn't be much biodiversity. But our planet has many, many environments. They include the icy poles and the hot tropics, deserts and rain forests, freshwater brooks and saltwater tide pools. Even our own backyards and neighborhoods have different environments and a variety of animals living in them. "To see our world as a space traveler might see it, for the first time...how utterly rich and wild it would seem," wrote Edward Abbey, an American author and environmentalist.

Today, about 1.5 million species of both animals and plants have been discovered and named. These include about four thousand mammals, nineteen thousand fishes, about nine thousand birds, and more than ten thousand reptiles and amphibians. The largest animal group by far is insects, with nearly eight hundred thousand named so far. And there are still many more species of animals to be discovered. Scientists estimate that there may be one million kinds in just one insect group, beetles. The total of all animal species on Earth may number several million.

Most of the animals still being discovered are insects, worms, and other small creatures without backbones, but larger animals are also found each year. In 1997, a squirrel-like mammal, the Panay cloudrunner, was first identified in the Philippines. Seven new species of monkeys were found in Brazil during the 1990s, as were two new kinds of electric fish in the Amazon River and a middle-sized deer in the forests of Vietnam.

Sadly, some of these newly-discovered animals exist only in very small numbers. They may become extinct before people can learn much about them. There are other wild animals in danger of extinction, too. What a loss it would be, to know that every single blue whale on Earth was gone, or that cheetahs would never again race across the African plains.

People can help prevent this from happening. A first step is simply to learn about the wonderful variety of animals on Earth—their names, their ways, and their connections with other living things. With knowledge comes caring. The beginnings of that knowledge and caring can be found in the pages of this book.

Alligator

(**al**-uh-gayt-uhr) An alligator is full of surprises. It may look like a gray or black log, limbs sprawled out at its sides, lying in the sun. Then it jumps up, with its legs straight under its body, and runs swiftly to grab an animal to eat. Small alligators eat insects, small fish, crabs, and crayfish. Really large alligators can be as long as a car (14 feet/4.3 meters), so they eat big fish, muskrats, birds, and turtles. Sometimes they grab deer or dogs. They rarely attack people.

There are only two kinds of alligators on Earth. One lives in parts of China, the other in the southeastern United States. The American alligator can be seen crossing roads, lawns, or golf courses. However, it spends most of its time in the water of ponds, canals, swamps, and rivers. It swims by swinging its long, powerful tail back and forth.

A female alligator is usually ten years old and 6 feet (1.8 meters) long when she is ready to **mate** and to lay eggs. She builds a nest of mud and plants. Near the top of the nest she lays several dozen eggs, then covers them. Sunshine and rotting plants in the nest provide the steady warm temperature the eggs need in order to **hatch**. The mother guards the nest. Baby alligators make chirping sounds when they are ready to hatch. Their mother guides them to water. She may carry some hatchlings in her mouth to the water, where she continues to guard them from harm.

Ant

(**ant**) No ant lives alone. Each one is a member of a colony, and each one has a job to do. Most ants are female workers. They build tunnels and mounds of earth, gather food, feed their young, and defend their colony.

More than fifteen thousand species of ants are known. This great variety includes carpenter ants that chew tunnels through wood, and leaf-cutting ants that parade back to their underground nests carrying bits of leaves they have cut. These ants eat fungus that grows on the decaying leaves. Other kinds of ants keep aphid "cows." The aphids suck sap from plants, then produce a sweet fluid that the ants drink. Other remarkable ants include army ants (shown here) that march in great numbers through rain forests, eating spiders, worms, and all sorts of insects, including other ants that do not flee in time.

Anteater

(**ant**-eet-uhr) Birds called flickers eat ants, armadillos eat ants, even bears eat ants, but anteaters eat ants every day, all year long. Anteaters also eat termites. Both ants and termites live by the thousands in **colonies**—a big meal for a hungry anteater.

Three kinds of anteaters live in the forests of Central and South America. The biggest species, 6 feet (1.8 meters) long, is called the giant anteater. It digs into ant and termite nests with its large, curved front claws. Then the anteater sticks its long snout into the colony and flicks out its sticky tongue. Any ant that is touched by the tongue gets stuck to it. To eat the ants, the anteater pulls its tongue back into its mouth and swallows them whole.

Armadillo

(ahr-muh-**dil**-oh) An armadillo seems to be made of parts from other animals. It has ears like a mule, a snout like a pig, a tail like a rat, and claws like a bear. It also has an armored body that reminds us of an ancient dinosaur. Its name means "little armored one" in Spanish.

About twenty kinds of armadillos live in South and Central America. Just one **species**—the nine-banded armadillo—lives in southern parts of the United States. It is about the size of a big house cat. Sadly, many people see these armadillos when they are dead, killed by cars or trucks on highways. When an armadillo is frightened or surprised it leaps into the air. This doesn't help it escape from an oncoming vehicle.

With their strong claws, armadillos dig burrows where they rest in the daytime. At night, they look for food on the ground—or underground. When an armadillo pokes its snout into the soil, it can smell ants, earthworms, or other prey several inches (centimeters) away. Its long tongue is covered with sticky saliva, so an armadillo can quickly slurp up dozens of ants.

An armadillo can swim well enough to cross rivers, but sometimes it holds its breath for as long as six minutes and simply walks across on the river bottom.

Baboon

(ba-**boon**) The face of a baboon reminds some people of a dog, but a baboon's eyes are close together and look straight ahead. It is a **primate**, related to monkeys, apes, and humans. Several kinds of baboons live in Africa, and are close relatives of mandrills and geladas.

The name baboon comes from an old French word for "lip." So the baboon was probably named for its rapid lip-smacking, a friendly signal among baboons. Small groups of baboons live together and sometimes join larger groups called troops. There may be more than one hundred baboons in a troop, which is led by the biggest males. Some of the other males act as scouts or rear guards, alert for an attack by a cheetah, leopard, or lion. Sometimes baboons and gazelles travel and feed together. The gazelles are alert with their sharp senses of smell and hearing. They warn others of danger with a shrill bark. The baboons stay alert with their keen eyesight and warn others of danger with a double bark.

Each morning the baboons set out to find food—mostly fruit, grains, flowers, and plant roots. Baboons may also eat bird eggs, grasshoppers, worms, and even scorpions. They learn to break off scorpions' stingers before putting the animals in their mouths.

Barnacle

(**bahr**-ni-kuhl) Anyone who visits the edge of the ocean can see a barnacle, or perhaps thousands of barnacles, on a rock. They are **crustaceans**, related to crabs and shrimp. Barnacles, however, do not move about in the sea. Except for a few weeks at the beginning of its life, a barnacle is stuck in one place. It makes a strong cement that withstands the most powerful waves and currents. Wherever it sticks itself, it opens parts of its tough outer shell and extends feathery "arms" that sweep bits of food from the passing water.

Many kinds of barnacles live in the world's oceans. Besides living on rocks, barnacles ride along on ship bottoms, on snail shells, on the bodies of crabs and whales, and even on the feet of penguins.

Bat

(**bat**) Bats are the only **mammals** that fly. Most bats rest in the daytime and hunt for food at night. This California leafnosed bat (shown here) was photographed as it was about to pluck a cricket from a cactus. Almost one thousand species of bats live on Earth, and most eat insects. Some fruit-eating bats that live in the tropics have wingspans of 6 feet (1.8 meters). These large bats have big eyes and foxlike faces, so they are often called flying foxes. Smaller bats have very small eyes, but are still able to find their way in the dark. As they fly, they make many calls and listen to echoes that return. From the echoes, bats are able to locate objects in front of them, including mosquitoes, moths, and other flying insects. Bats eat many insects that are pests to people or damage plants that produce food.

Bear

(**bair**) Some people think of bears as animal monsters—big, powerful, dangerous. Bears are big and powerful, but rarely hurt humans. Even the grizzly bear of North America (shown here) usually avoids people. Hikers in grizzly bear country are urged to ring a bell or make other noise to warn bears away.

Of the eight bear species on Earth, the polar bear is the biggest. In fact, it is the world's largest land predator. Males can weigh nearly 1 ton (0.9 tonne) and stand 11 feet (3.3 meters) tall. Polar bears swim several miles (kilometers) from shore, and roam Arctic ice, hunting seals. The most common North American bear—the black bear—usually weighs no more than 500 pounds (227 kilograms). It is a good climber. Its claws are more curved than those of a grizzly, which cannot climb trees.

Bears are **omnivores**, eating both plants and animals. Black bears and grizzlies eat everything from dead animal carcasses to ants, but eat mostly grass, roots, nuts, and berries. As summer advances toward autumn, bears become "hungry as a bear!" They eat as much as possible, storing fat that will help them live through months without food. Snug in a winter den, they slip into a deep sleep called hibernation. In the spring they wake up much thinner and very hungry.

Beaver

(**bee**-vuhr) Beavers are builders. Using parts of trees, mud, and stones, they build a dam across a stream. The water rises and spreads out behind the dam, creating a pond. Cutting more trees with their sharp teeth, the beavers build a wooden shelter, called a lodge, in the water. Both the lodge and the water of the pond help protect beavers from coyotes and other predators that might attack them on land. By creating ponds, beavers also affect many other living things. When a pond forms, forest plants die and forest animals may have to move, but frogs, fish, water lilies, and other pond life thrives.

The beaver is a **rodent**, related to mice, squirrels, and chipmunks. It is the largest rodent in North America, sometimes weighing as much as 70 pounds (31.5 kilograms). It has an unusual tail, flat and scaly, which helps push the beaver through the water when it swims. When a beaver smacks its tail on the water surface, it makes a loud noise and warns other beavers of possible danger. For safety, they dive and swim to an underwater entrance to their lodge.

In the late summer and fall, beavers cut many tree branches and make a pile of them in the water near their lodge. Then, in the winter, when ice may cover the pond's surface, the beavers swim under the ice to this food pile and bring branches into the lodge. Tree bark is their main food in winter.

Bee

(**bee**) The bumblebee (shown here) will sip a sweet liquid called nectar from the flower. Tiny grains of the flower's pollen will stick to its body and legs. When the bee moves from one flower to another, it carries pollen to each flower. This process is called **pollination**. Without pollination, many kinds of plants would not produce fruits and other foods.

Most kinds of bees live alone, but bumblebees and honeybees live in colonies. Each colony has a single queen that lays eggs. A queen honeybee usually lays thousands of eggs, most of which develop into female worker bees. They are well named: Worker bees defend their colony with their stingers, make wax and build honeycombs, and make honey from flower nectar.

Beetle

(**beet**-l) Beetles are by far the most numerous and varied group of insects. About three hundred thousand species are known, and new kinds of beetles are discovered each year. Insects with other names—ladybugs, fireflies, June bugs—are all beetles. The boll weevil, a pest of cotton plants, is actually a snout beetle. Several kinds of beetles have one or more horns on their heads. They include stag and rhinoceros beetles. They look fierce, but are harmless plant eaters. Beetles come in a great variety of sizes, shapes, and colors, but they all have the same four stages of life: egg, larva (sometimes called a grub), pupa, and adult.

Bison

(**bie**-suhn) More than four hundred years ago, Spanish explorers in North America saw vast herds of grazing animals. These big creatures seemed to have horns like cows, manes like lions, and humps on their shoulders like camels. Today many people call these animals "buffalo," but they are not like the buffalo that live in Asia and Africa. They are bison, the largest land animals in North America. One variety, the wood bison, lives only in Canada. It is darker and bigger than the plains bison that lives in both Canada and the United States. Both varieties of bison grow a thick, shaggy coat of hair in winter. And both male and female bison grow

horns. The horns of a male (bull) bison can be as long as 26 inches (65 centimeters).

Bison provided Native Americans of the Great Plains with many of their needs, including food, shelter, and clothing. Bison bones were made into tools, and dried bison droppings were used as fuel when firewood was scarce. Bison ribs were made into runners of sleds used by Native American children. In the early 1700s, as many as sixty million bison roamed North America. Then, explorers and settlers from European countries began to take over the continent. They nearly wiped out the bison. By 1890, only a few hundred remained. They were protected in parks and zoos, and their numbers have grown. Today, about 250,000 bison roam on ranches and in large western parks, including Yellowstone National Park in the United States and Wood Buffalo National Park in Canada.

Butterfly

(**buht**-uhr-flie) The life of a new butterfly begins when its mother lays an egg on the leaf of a plant. A tiny caterpillar hatches from the egg. It takes little bites from leaves and grows bigger. One day, the caterpillar makes a protective sack called a **chrysalis**. The caterpillar goes through many changes inside the chrysalis. When the chrysalis splits open, a butterfly climbs out.

At first, its wings look small and weak, but they soon unfold and grow bigger and stronger. The butterfly flexes its wings up and down, then lets go with its feet and begins to fly. Soon, it lands on a flower, where it uncoils a long drinking tube and sips sweet nectar from the blossom.

Butterflies are among the most beautiful and beloved of all insects. Some are as small as a penny, while others measure 6 inches (15 centimeters) across. Late in the summer, monarch butterflies (shown here) begin to fly south from Canada and all over the United States. Monarchs west of the Rocky Mountains fly to cool resting places in southern California. East of the Rockies, monarchs may fly more than 2,000 miles (3,219 kilometers) to mountaintop forests in central Mexico. In the spring, they mate and produce a new generation of monarchs that flies to the north.

Camel

(**kam**-uhl) Camels are sometimes called "ships of the desert" because they can carry heavy loads and are good desert travelers. Camels have wide, padded feet that do not sink far into sand. They have long eyelashes and special eyelids that protect their eyes from windblown sand. They can shut their nostrils to keep sand out of their noses. Camels can also go many days without water. The leaves of living plants contain water, so camels get some of the water they need simply by eating. They stay alert for the scent of water, which their keen sense of smell can detect from miles (kilometers) away. Once a camel reaches water, it can drink 50 gallons (189 liters) in one day.

Many people believe that camels store water in the humps on their backs. Actually, camel humps are lumps of stored fat, a reserve supply of energy if food becomes scarce. The number of humps on a camel's back is a good clue to its identity. Asian camels, also called Bactrian camels, have two humps. Arabian camels (shown here) are from northern Africa and have one hump. A special variety of Arabian camel called the dromedary is bred for racing. Most Arabian camels are not racers, but are valued for their steady walking pace while carrying people and heavy loads through the desert.

Canary

(kuh-**ner**-ee) West of Morocco in northern Africa lie the Canary Islands. On these islands live small greenish-yellow wild birds. Many centuries ago, people who liked the sweet songs of these birds discovered that they were easily tamed. Eventually, these birds became popular pets all over the world, but they are named after their original home—the Canaries.

Many canaries are yellow. However, by choosing certain canaries and allowing them to mate, people have produced white, green, blue, and light red varieties, and some with crests and frills. Each variety of canary sings a different song. Only the males sing. They are trained to sing by listening to older birds or to music in the home where they live.

Cardinal

(**kahrd**-n-uhl) The cardinal is sometimes called a "redbird," and there is no other red bird like it. Except for some black feathers on its face, a male cardinal (shown here) is all red. Its crest of feathers is red, and so is its stout beak. A female cardinal is colored brownish-pink.

The cardinal once lived mostly in the South but slowly spread northward. Now it can be found as far north as southern Canada. Cardinals do not migrate south in the autumn, as many other songbirds do. Cardinals eat insects, berries, and a variety of seeds. In winter, many people put sunflower seeds, a favorite cardinal food, in bird feeders.

Caribou

(**kair**-uh-boo) A herd of caribou sometimes looks like a moving forest because both males and females have antlers. The antlers, up to 5 feet (1.5 meters) across, look like twigs and branches of trees. Antlers help caribou defend themselves and their young against wolves.

Caribou are members of the deer family and live in the far north. The caribou of Siberia and Scandanavia are called reindeer. In North America there are several kinds of caribou. Those that live farthest north are called barren-ground caribou (shown here). Another name for the barren, tree-less lands of the Arctic is **tundra**.

Grasses, lichens, and other low-growing plants cover the tundra. Caribou eat these plants, even when snow covers the ground. The name caribou comes from a Native American word that means "snow shoveler," because caribou scrape away snow with their broad hooves to uncover their food.

In the fall, vast herds of barren-ground caribou travel hundreds of miles (kilometers) south to their winter range. They **migrate** back north in the spring. They climb mountains and cross rivers, following ancient migration routes.

Cat

(kat) Few people get to see a wild tiger or lion stalk its prey, but you can see the same behavior, on a smaller scale, by watching house cats or kittens at play. They creep low along the floor, eyes on their play partner, then spring forward to attack. One reason for the great popularity of cats as pets is the way they resemble their wild relatives. Cats are agile and graceful. They are also affectionate, clean, and easy to care for.

A cat can sleep sixteen hours a day. In fact, cats are such good sleepers that a person's short nap is called a "catnap." And cats are such good climbers that a thief who climbs to rob a

home is called a "cat burglar." Cats are often active at night. They see well in dim light, and they can also feel their way in the dark, helped by touch-sensitive whiskers on their faces and front legs. Cats also have a keen sense of hearing. They can move each ear independently, aiming it in the direction of a sound.

The position of a cat's ears, the position and motions of its tail, and the sounds it makes are all clues to its mood. Many people enjoy learning about these clues as they share their home with a cat. Most of all, they like to hear the sound of a contented cat—a purr.

Centipede

(**sent**-uh-peed) The name centipede means "hundred legs." Of the three thousand kinds of centipedes in the world, most do not have one hundred legs, but some have more than three hundred. Centipedes have flat bodies and can squeeze into narrow spaces under rocks and pieces of wood.

Centipedes can move fast to escape enemies or to hunt for insects, earthworms, and other small animals. The biggest centipedes, some 12 inches (30 centimeters) long, can kill mice and lizards. Centipedes sting their prey with poisonous fangs. The fangs of most small centipedes are too small to pierce human skin, but if they do, even the smallest centipede can give you a painful sting.

Chameleon

(kuh-**meel**-yuhn) The three-horned chameleon (shown here) has just flicked out its long, sticky tongue to capture a cricket. Just as quickly, the tongue will pull back into the chameleon's mouth and the cricket will be swallowed. Then the chameleon will rest on its branch, watching for another meal. Its two eyes can look in different directions at the same time. Another unusual characteristic of chameleons is their ability to change color. They often change

color slowly, but under some circumstances can make dramatic changes in less than fifteen seconds. A chameleon changing quickly from a solid color to a striped or spotted pattern is an amazing sight.

So far, 128 species of chameleons are known, mostly in Africa and in Madagascar, a big island east of Africa.

Cheetah

(**cheet**-uh) The cheetah is Earth's fastest land animal. It is built for speed, with a small head, slender body, and long, powerful legs. For a short time, a cheetah may be able to reach speeds up to 70 miles (113 kilometers) an hour. Sometimes it needs to run this fast to escape from a lion or other **predator** on the open plains of Africa. More often, it races to catch a rabbit, gazelle, or impala. If the cheetah gets close enough, it strikes its prey with a front paw, knocking it over. Then the cheetah clamps its jaws on the animal's throat, cutting off its air supply.

The cheetah drags its **prey** to a hiding place. However, lions, hyenas, and vultures often force a cheetah to leave its prey before it has finished eating. A cheetah mother also must protect its young from lions, leopards, and hyenas. Every few days, she moves her cubs to a new hideout.

Cheetahs once lived over much of Africa, the Middle East, and India. Now fewer than ten thousand survive in parts of southern and eastern Africa. Their favorite habitat of **savanna**—grassland with scattered trees—is being changed to farmland. There is still hope that the swift and beautiful cheetah will survive in parks and other large reserves.

Chicken

(**chik**-uhn) In the wilds of India and Southeast Asia live small ground-feeding birds called red jungle fowl (shown here). About five thousand years ago, people tamed some jungle fowl, and they are the ancestors of the birds we call chickens. Meat and eggs from chickens are an important source of food worldwide.

In the United States alone, people eat more than three billion chickens and eggs from 280 million hens each year. Hens are adult female chickens. A hen can produce about twenty dozen eggs a year.

By mating birds with different characteristics, people have produced chickens that are much bigger than jungle fowl. The white leghorn, which has white feathers, is the most common breed in North America. White

leghorn hens also lay white eggs. Some other varieties of chicken, including the Plymouth Rock and the Rhode Island Red, produce brown eggs. It usually takes about one day for a complete egg to develop within a hen's body.

Chickens are social animals that form a "pecking order" when allowed to interact in a flock. This means that each bird yields to those above it in rank and "bosses" those below it. Adult male chickens are called roosters, or cocks. A rooster has a showy growth on top of its head called a comb, and one under its chin called a wattle. Roosters are famous for their loud *cock-a-doodle-do* calls given at the first hint of daylight. They are one of nature's alarm clocks.

Chimpanzee

(chimp-pan-**zee**) At one time, people thought that only humans were smart enough to use tools. Then chimpanzees were seen making and using simple tools to get food or water. To catch termites to eat, a chimpanzee chooses a short twig and peels off its leaves. Then the chimp pokes the twig into an underground termite nest. After waiting a short while for termites to grab onto the twig, the chimp pulls the twig out and eats the termites. Only the most intelligent mammals and birds use tools. Chimpanzees are primates, closely related to orangutans, gorillas, and humans. Another close relative is the bonobo, which used to be called the pygmy chimpanzee.

Chimpanzees live in groups and are very social animals. They communicate with one another by sounds, facial expressions, and by smell and touch. Chimpanzees make at least thirty-four different sounds. Some of their facial expressions have meanings that are different from human expressions. When a chimpanzee gives a big, toothy smile, it is afraid, not happy.

Chimpanzees live in African forests, where they search for plant and animal food by day, and make tree nests for nighttime sleep. Like gorillas and orangutans, chimpanzees cannot survive in the wild if large areas of their forest **habitat** are not saved.

Chipmunk

(**chip**-muhngk) Known for their "chipping" calls, striped coats, and alert ways, chipmunks are appealing little rodents. They are ground squirrels, related to many kinds of ground squirrels that live in western North America. Eastern chipmunks, which live in eastern North America, are about 8 to 10 inches (20 to 25 centimeters) long, with their bushy tails making up nearly half of that length. There are about a dozen species of chipmunks in western North America. They include the cliff chipmunk, Colorado chipmunk, and least chipmunk. On their backs, all chipmunks have five dark stripes separated by four light-colored ones.

Although chipmunks sometimes climb trees in search of nuts and seeds, they are usually seen scampering on the forest floor, or watching and listening from the top of a log or a stone wall. If a chipmunk senses

danger, it dashes for safety, diving into a tunnel it has dug. The tunnel usually leads to a nest of leaves, storerooms for food, and other tunnels that lead to the surface. During the winter, chipmunks sleep in their nests, but they need a store of food in the early spring. Their storerooms are filled with nuts and seeds gathered in the fall. One chipmunk was seen collecting and storing nearly one thousand acorns in one day. A chipmunk can carry many seeds at once in its cheek pouches. As it puts seed after seed in its mouth, its cheeks bulge out farther and farther. When they are fully loaded, the chipmunk scurries to its underground home.

Cichlid

(**sik**-lid) Fish called cichlids are an extraordinary group. More than one thousand species of cichlids live in the freshwater lakes and rivers of Africa, Madagascar, India, and Latin America. Cichlids are popular aquarium fish, partly because they are so smart. Some aquarium-keepers claim that cichlids can recognize different people who visit their fish tank. Cichlids are also noted for the care that they give to their young. In many species, the female cichlid keeps fertilized eggs in her mouth for about three weeks. She goes without food until they hatch. This is called mouthbrooding. When the baby fish, called fry, emerge from their eggs, she releases them into the water. However, she stays near the fry until they can fend for themselves. They dart back into her mouth at the first sign of danger. In some cichlid species, the parent fish feed their young by allowing them to nibble at the scales and mucus cells on the surface of their bodies.

Wild cichlids are amazingly varied in their size, color, and ways of life. Some are as large as a goat, others as small as a penny. Some eat plants, others are predators. One species looks like a decaying fish. It often floats in the water, looking dead. When another fish approaches for an easy meal, the cichlid attacks and gets a meal instead.

Clam

(**klam**) Clams spend most of their lives in one place. Many kinds of clams also stay hidden in sand or mud. Clams are **mollusks**, related to snails and oysters. Among mollusks, clams are part of a group called **bivalves**, which means they are protected by two shells that fit together snugly. There is a hinge on one side so the two shells can open and close.

A clam can dig by opening its two shells to extend its muscular foot. To eat, a clam extends two siphons that reach out of the mud or sand and filter bits of food from the water. When a clam is not digging or feeding, it withdraws its siphons and foot, then tightens two strong muscles that hold its two shells closed. The whole clam animal inside its shells is considered to be delicious by many people, so clams are often eaten in soups and sauces.

Giant clams (shown here) live in the Pacific and Indian Oceans. They are the largest and most beautiful clams in the world, sometimes weighing ¼ ton (0.23 tonne). One giant clamshell is big enough to be used as a child's bathtub. Giant clams do not hide beneath the seafloor. They are often part of a coral reef. There are tales that giant clams have closed on the arms or feet of divers, trapping them and causing them to drown, but there is no proof that this has ever happened.

Coral

(**kor**-uhl) Corals were once thought to be plants. Like plants, they stay in one place for nearly all of their lives, but corals are predatory animals. A single coral is called a polyp. Its mouth is ringed with tentacles that are armed with stinging cells. Tiny animals that drift within reach are stung, grabbed, and swallowed by the coral polyp.

Many coral animals have the ability to take minerals from the water and make a protective skeleton of limestone. These hard corals live in colonies. Through the years, the life and death of countless coral colonies leaves an underwater landscape called a coral reef. A reef has a foundation of limestone, covered with a variety of living coral colonies. Coral reefs thrive in sunlit, warm salt water. Earth's biggest reef is the Great Barrier Reef, which is actually made up of about three thousand reefs that stretch along Australia's northeastern coast.

Coral reefs have been called the "rain forests of the sea" because they are homes for such a variety of life: fish, crabs, sponges, sea stars, sea urchins, shrimps, and anemones. Corals themselves total about 2,500 species. Some are soft corals, which do not form reefs. They include sea fans and sea plumes. The hard coral colonies that build reefs include brain coral (shown here), staghorn coral, and one called dead man's fingers. Each of these colonies is made up of many coral animals.

Cow

(kou) Got milk? Got ice cream, cheese, yogurt, cream, butter? None of these foods would be so plentiful in our lives without cows. We can make cheese and other dairy foods from the milk of goats, but cows, being much larger, can produce great quantities of milk. One cow can yield 35 quarts (33 liters) or more of milk a day.

When we see these dairy animals grazing in a pasture, we usually call them cows, but a more accurate name is cattle. Grown-up female cattle are cows. Grown-up males are bulls. There are just two species of cattle in the world, but many different varieties have been produced. Breeds called Angus and Hereford are raised as beef animals, which are usually called steers (shown here). Their muscles become steaks, hamburger, and other meat products. Most dairy cows are of the black-and-white Holstein breed, although there are other brown-colored dairy breeds, including Jersey and Guernsey. (No, it is *not* true that brown cows produce chocolate milk!)

Cattle have four-chambered stomachs that allow them to quickly gulp down grass and other plant foods without much chewing. Later, muscles force chunks of grass back up into the mouth to be chewed. Hours after a cow grazed you may see it "chewing its cud," as this process is called.

Coyote

(kie-**oht**-ee) or (**kie**-oht) The coyote is a wild member of the dog family living in North America. Native Americans of the Great Plains called it "the trickster," and admired its intelligence. The coyote has also been called "the song dog," because of the rich variety of sounds it makes. Coyote calls include the yelp, woof, bark, bark-yip, lone howl, group howl, group howl-yip, and a greeting song.

The coyote is also called the "brush wolf," although it is usually less than one-half the size of a wolf. Unlike the wolf, which needs a large wilderness habitat, the coyote adapts to all sorts of habitats. Even though the coyote can be hunted and trapped, it continues to thrive all over North America. It has spread south of Mexico and north to Alaska and northern Canada. Coyotes have been seen within the limits of Los Angeles, New York, and many other cities.

A predator, the coyote will kill and eat whatever animals it can catch, including mice, ground squirrels, gophers, lizards, rabbits, sheep, and even pet dogs and cats. If grapes, berries, cactus fruit, or grasshoppers are abundant, a coyote will feast on them, too.

Crab

(**crab**) When you walk along the seashore you often see crabs. However, in some areas you can see crabs on land, and even high up in trees. Coconut crabs can climb up 50 feet (15.2 meters) to feed on the fruit of coconut trees. All over the world there are many kinds of crabs—

more than five thousand species. Spider crabs live deep in the ocean. They may measure 12 feet (3.7 meters) from the tip of one skinny leg to the opposite tip. In contrast, a fullgrown pea crab measures just ¼ inch (1 centimeter) across. Crabs are colorful, fascinating crustaceans, related to lobsters and shrimp. They include stone crabs (shown here), ghost crabs, fiddler crabs, calico crabs, and the bright red Sally Lightfoot crab that lives on the shores of the Galápagos Islands.

Cricket

(**krik**-it) *Chirp . . . Chirp . . . Chirp!* The sound of crickets chirping reminds many people of a quiet evening in the country. In Asia, crickets are kept as pets so people can enjoy their music at home. Only male crickets chirp. They produce loud sounds by rubbing the underside of one front wing against the upper side of the opposite wing. Males

make three different sounds. One is a fighting challenge to another male, and the second claims a **territory** and attracts females. The third chirp is a gentle courtship song. Both female and male crickets can hear these sounds with the simple "ears" on their front legs.

Crocodile

(**krahk**-uh-dile) Crocodiles seem to smile. Even with their jaws closed they have a toothy grin. Crocodiles have narrow, pointy snouts, while their close relatives, alligators, have wider, more rounded snouts. Crocodiles called gavials have long, slender snouts shaped like birds' beaks. All crocodiles have sharp teeth set in powerful jaws, and catch other animals for food.

Just one kind of crocodile (shown here) lives in the United States. Only about 450 of these American crocodiles survive in southern Florida. They sometimes swim in the salty water at the edge of the Gulf of Mexico.

The biggest crocodiles of all are saltwater crocodiles. "Salties," as they are sometimes called, may measure more than 20 feet (6.1 meters) long and weigh 1 ton (0.9 tonne). They live along some coasts of Australia, New Guinea, and Indonesia. Although most crocodiles avoid people, big saltwater crocodiles sometimes attack swimmers—and even small boats. Many tourists who visit northern Australia want to see saltwater crocodiles, so they are given safety tips to help them avoid trouble.

Crow

(**kroh**) *Caw! Caw! Caw!* The call of a crow is bold and sassy. It is the voice of a highly successful bird that is smart enough to adapt to many different situations. It can live well in wilderness or in a world of shopping malls and city parks. Actually, crows say much more than *caw*. They have about twenty-five different calls, including rattles, growls, and coos. They can imitate the sounds of other birds and human voices.

One sign of their intelligence is playfulness. Young crows play tug-of-war with sticks, and can drop a stick in the air, and then zoom down to catch it before it hits the ground. Crows are also clever at getting food. After watching ice fishermen pull fish through holes cut in ice, a crow may take over where a fishing line is left untended. It pulls the line up through the hole, then eats the bait or the fish that is on the hook.

A pair of crows usually mates for life. They have plenty of helpers in raising their young. Crows born a year or two earlier bring food for the mother and nestlings and stand guard by the nest. When a crow sees an owl, hawk, cat, or other predator, it gives an alarm call. This often brings in dozens of other crows. The air is filled with a loud crow chorus. This behavior is called mobbing. Crows are sometimes chased and mobbed by smaller birds, too.

Deer

(**dir**) The fawn of a white-tailed deer (shown here) is hidden in the woods. Its spotted coat blends in well with the sun-dappled forest floor. It waits quietly for its mother to return.

Female deer, called does, often have twin fawns, so deer numbers can grow quickly. Today, deer are the most common large wild animals in North America. They are more plentiful now than they were when the continent was originally settled by people from Europe. Although deer live in the wild countryside, they can also thrive in the habitat of open spaces and patches of woodland they find in some suburbs. Having lots of deer around is a mixed blessing. People admire their grace and beauty, but deer eat food crops, flowers, and other valuable plants.

Forty different kinds of deer live on Earth. The pudu deer of the mountains of Chile is only 13 inches (33 centimeters) tall. In the United States, the white-tailed deer is the most common species east of the Rocky Mountains. West of the Rockies the mule deer is most common. It is named for its big, wide, mule-like ears. Each summer, bucks, as males are called, grow antlers on their heads. The antlers drop off after deer mating season, and a new pair grows the following year.

33

Dog (**dawg**) or (**dahg**) It is hard to believe that all dogs belong to the same species. They come in such a variety of sizes, shapes, and colors. Different breeds of dogs include the Newfoundland and Saint Bernard, which can weigh as much as a man, and the tiny Chihuahua, which weighs no more than 6 pounds (2.7 kilograms). Nevertheless, scientists believe that all dogs have a common ancestor: the wolf. Over thousands of years, peo-

ple picked certain dogs for mating with other dogs, aiming for pups with specific characteristics. This is called **selective breeding**.

The result is not just different-looking dogs, but also dogs that have special skills. There are big breeds that guard sheep, and smaller ones that herd sheep. There are also breeds that are good at hunting and retrieving birds on land, and others that can swim and retrieve ducks. All dogs have a highly developed sense of smell, and the bloodhound is one breed that is used to follow scent trails and locate missing people. Dogs can also hear sounds that human ears cannot detect.

In the United States, there is about one dog for every three people. In many ways, however, these popular pets still behave like their ancient ancestors. Male dogs leave scent marks of urine on trees and other objects. Wolves do the same to mark the borders of their territories.

Dolphin

(**dahl**-fin) or (**dawl**-fin) All dolphins are toothed whales. There are about thirty-two species worldwide. The biggest is the killer whale. Some dolphin species live far out in the ocean, others closer to shore, and some swim far upstream in rivers, including the Amazon in South America and the Yangtze in China. The species most familiar to people is the bottlenose dolphin (shown here) because it is the kind trained to perform in aquarium shows. Since dolphins are highly intelligent, they can be taught all sorts of complicated tricks.

Since they are mammals, not fish, dolphins must rise to the surface every few minutes for a breath of air. They breathe through an opening in the top of their heads that closes when they dive underwater. There they hunt for food, including fish, crabs, and squid. Dolphins have no jaw muscles for chewing. They grab a fish with their teeth, then swallow it whole. A large male bottlenose dolphin may eat as many as 30 pounds (13.5 kilograms) of fish a day.

Bottlenose dolphins sometimes leap far out of the water as they play. Dolphins are very social animals. They communicate with one another through a "language" of clicks, chirps, and whistles. They also locate objects and find their way underwater by listening to echoes of sounds they make.

Dragonfly

(**drag**-uhn-flie) A dragonfly can hover in the air like a helicopter, then quickly zoom along at 30 miles (48 kilometers) an hour. It can dart to the side, fly backward, and turn a somersault. The flying ability of dragonflies is admired and studied by engineers who design aircraft. Nevertheless, most dragonflies spend more of their life underwater than in the air. Female dragonflies lay eggs in or near streams, ponds, or other wetlands. The nymphs that hatch from the eggs feed and grow underwater. They are predators, catching and eating other insects, and sometimes tadpoles and snails.

After months or even years underwater, a dragonfly nymph climbs out, its skin splits open, and an adult dragonfly emerges. Once its wings spread out and dry, its life in the air begins. Most dragonflies stay in one area all of their lives, though a few species can migrate more than 1,000 miles (1,600 kilometers).

Some people believe that dragonflies have stingers and can hurt people, but they are harmless—and very helpful. Dragonflies may have the sharpest vision of all insects, and are especially good at spotting insects on the move. They catch so many mosquitoes that they are often called mosquito hawks. Sometimes a dragonfly darts in to pluck a bloodsucking mosquito or a biting black fly right from a person's skin!

Duck

(**duhk**) Ducks walk with short steps that tilt their bodies from side to side. This is called waddling. Though awkward on land, ducks are swift fliers and strong swimmers. Their webbed feet act like paddles, propelling them through the water. Some kinds of ducks can dive more than 100 feet (30.5 meters) beneath the surface. A duck's feathers do not get wet because they are coated with oil. The duck takes the oil from a special gland near its tail and spreads it on with its bill.

In North America, the most familiar wild duck is the mallard. The male mallard (shown here) is more colorful than the female (which is true of most birds). Mallards are dabbling ducks. They feed in shallow water and dip their heads under to feed on the leaves, stems, and seeds of plants, and also snails and insects below the surface. Other dabblers

include teals, pintails, and widgeons. They leap into the air to take flight.

Diving ducks need to run along the water's surface to take flight. They dive underwater to feed on crabs and other small animals. Some divers spend their winters in protected bays, while others, called eiders and scoters, can be found far out in the ocean. Other kinds of diving ducks, called mergansers, have saw-edged bills that grasp the slippery fish they catch to eat.

Eagle

(**ee**-guhl) Eagles are big, powerful birds. There are sixty-six species on Earth. Throughout history, the eagle has been used as a symbol of strength on battle shields, coins, and national flags. The bald eagle (shown here), one of two eagle species in North America, is the national bird of the United States. Of course, this eagle is not really bald. Its head and tail feathers are normally white once it reaches about five years of age.

With a wingspan of up to 8 feet (2.4 meters) the bald eagle is slightly bigger than the golden eagle, which is most abundant in the West. Golden eagles catch most of their food, including rabbits and mice, on land. Bald eagles mostly eat fish, so they are often found near rivers and large lakes. They soar above the water, watching for a big fish

near the surface. Eagle eyes are much stronger than human eyes. When a bald eagle spots a fish, it folds its wings and plunges toward the water. Clutching a fish in its sharp **talons**, the eagle carries its catch to a tree and begins to rip off bites with its hooked beak. Bald eagles also catch ducks and eat dead fish that wash ashore. Both golden and bald eagles are protected by law. Their survival depends on having safe places for their giant nests and having wild places to roam.

Eel (**eel**) The long, slender bodies of eels remind some people of snakes or worms, but eels are a kind of fish. Like all fish, eels have fins and a bony skeleton. They breathe by means of gills and through their skin, which is usually covered with tiny scales. Eels have very flexible bodies and a slimy coating of mucus on their skin. When people want to describe something that is almost impossible to hold, they say "It's as slippery as an eel."

More than six hundred species of eels are known. Most live in the ocean. They include snake eels (shown here), worm eels, gulper eels, conger eels, and moray eels. The giant moray is the largest of all known eels. It can grow to be 10 feet (3 meters) long. Garden eels live by the hundreds in colonies on the seafloor. Each eel rises out of its burrow but leaves its tail inside. As the eels eat small animals from the water, they look like a garden of plants swaying in the current.

Some female eels live and grow for several years in freshwater streams and rivers. Then they swim downstream and far out in the ocean, where they mate with male eels and produce a new generation of young.

Elephant

(**el**-uh-fuhnt) Long ago, many kinds of elephants, including woolly mammoths, lived on Earth. Now just two kinds remain: Asian and African elephants. The Asian elephant stands 10 feet (3 meters) high at its shoulder and lives in the forests of India, Sri Lanka, and Southeast Asia. Asian elephants have been tamed to carry people, lift heavy logs, and perform in circuses.

The African elephant (shown here) is even bigger, standing as tall as 13 feet (4 meters) at its shoulder. It lives mostly in a savanna habitat of grassland with scattered trees. It often walks 10 miles (16 kilometers) a day or more in search of food, and eats 200 pounds (91 kilograms) or more of grasses, berries, bark, twigs, and other plant foods daily. An elephant brings food to its mouth with its long, muscular trunk. With nostrils at the end of its trunk, an elephant can smell food or water from miles (kilometers) away. With the tip of its trunk, an elephant can pluck fruit from high overhead or pick a peanut off the ground. An elephant can also suck water into its trunk to give itself a drink—or a shower.

Elephants live in family groups led by the older females. People are working to help save wild lands where these gentle and intelligent animals can survive.

Finch

(**finch**) The male zebra finch (shown here) gets its name from the zebralike stripes on its throat and chest. Popular as a pet, it is originally from Australia. Zebra finches are just one of 153 finch species worldwide. Almost all finches have stout, cone-shaped beaks used to crack open seeds. The finch family includes the chaffinch and greenfinch, which are common wild birds in

Europe. In North America, the best-known finch is the goldfinch. This species lines its nest with the soft downy material that develops within thistle flowers. Goldfinches do not mate or begin nest building until late summer, when thistledown becomes available.

Firefly

(**fire**-flie) As darkness falls on a summer night, tiny lights wink on and off over lawns and bushes. The lights move through the air, then disappear. These magical, mysterious lights are made by fireflies, which are also called lightning bugs. These insects are neither flies nor bugs, they are beetles. Even before they become adult beetles, the **larvae** of fireflies sometimes give off light. They are called glowworms.

Chemicals mixed together in a firefly's body produce light, called **bioluminescence**. Firefly lights are mating signals. Each species of firefly has its own code, or special pattern of flashes, that enables males and females of that species to find one another.

Flamingo

(fluh-**ming**-goh) The flamingo is the tallest water bird on Earth. The biggest species, called the American or greater flamingo, can grow to be more than 5 feet (1.5 meters) tall. When it flies with its long neck and slender legs stretched straight out, a flamingo looks like a flying stick.

Flamingos make nest mounds of mud that look like short tree stumps. Usually only one egg is laid on top of the mound, and both parents take turns keeping it warm. When flamingo chicks hatch, their beaks are straight. As they grow bigger, their beaks begin to curve downward into a hooked shape, like their parents'.

Newly hatched flamingo chicks are covered with soft white down feathers. As they grow, their first suit of new feathers is gray. Later, some new feathers are pink or red. Fully grown flamingos are orange-red, with black on their beak tips and the back edges of their wings. However, a flamingo's color is affected by its food. A flamingo feeds by straining water and mud through its beak, separating out little snails, shrimp, and brine flies that live in salty water. This diet gives wild flamingos their rosy color. Given other food, a flamingo's colors may fade to gray.

Fly

(**flie**) Flies are unusual insects because they have only one pair of wings. All true flies are members of a group called Diptera, which means "two wings." However, flies also have a pair of unusual clublike balancing organs. Having these and two wings enables flies to fly swiftly, turn somersaults, and do other aerial tricks. Although mos-

quitoes are classified as flies, the best-known member of the Diptera is the housefly. It feeds on all sorts of food. Before landing on some picnic food, a housefly may have fed on garbage, manure, or the remains of a dead animal. Germs spread by houseflies have caused outbreaks of disease. Many other kinds of flies are harmless, or even beneficial. They include the flower fly (shown here), crane fly, robber fly, and dance fly.

Frog

(**frawg**) or (**frahg**) If someone asked you to make a noise like a frog, you would probably say "*croak*," or "*ribbit*." There are so many kinds of frogs, however, you would be correct to bark, grunt, honk, peep, or twang, too. You could also give a deep *jug-o-rum* sound—the call of a bullfrog. Male frogs make these sounds in mating season, when frogs gather in ponds, swamps, and other wetlands. Frogs are **amphibians**. Female frogs must lay their eggs in water. Tiny creatures, called tadpoles or pollywogs, hatch from the eggs. As they grow, four legs sprout from their bodies, their tails shrink and disappear, and lungs develop for breathing out of the water. Adult frogs have big, powerful hind legs, built for fast swimming and giant leaps. A leopard frog (shown here) can jump 5 feet (1.5 meters) —twelve times its length.

Gerbil

(**juhr**-buhl) In the deserts of Africa and Asia live many different kinds of gerbils, small rodents with long tails. They are most active at night, when it is cool. In the daytime, gerbils avoid the desert heat and rest in their underground burrows. Since they live in deserts, where water is scarce, gerbils get most of the water they need from within the seeds and other plant foods they eat.

In 1935, about twenty pairs of gerbils were captured alive in Mongolia, a desert area north of China. Those Mongolian gerbils were allowed to breed and produce young. For a while gerbils were used only for scientific studies in laboratories, but people noticed that gerbils had qualities that would make them good pets. Gerbils are curious, lively, gentle, clean, and easily tamed. Today countless homes have pet gerbils. They differ from wild gerbils because they are usually active in the day and sleep at night. Gerbils make two sounds: tiny squeaks and a drumming sound males make with their hind feet. Most pet gerbils are the same tan color as their wild relatives in Mongolia. However, animal breeders have picked certain odd-colored gerbils for breeding and have produced gerbils of several colors, including black, white, and gray.

Giraffe

(juh-**raf**) The giraffe is Earth's tallest animal. Its neck alone is as tall as an average-sized man, 6 feet (1.8 meters). Some male giraffes tower 19 feet (5.8 meters) in the air—tall enough to peer over the tops of many houses. Giraffes are able to feed from high bushes and from treetops that other animals cannot reach. They especially like the leaves of acacia trees that are scattered on the plains of central and southern Africa, where many giraffes live. A giraffe plucks leaves from acacia trees with its 18-inch-(46-centimeter) long tongue. Its tongue and mouth have a thick coating of mucus that protects the giraffe from acacia thorns.

A giraffe's height helps it see far over the countryside. It watches for lions, which sometimes attack giraffes.

However, being tall is bothersome for a giraffe when it needs water. At the edge of a water hole, a giraffe cannot drink until it spreads its front legs far apart so its mouth can reach the water.

A giraffe calf can run just a few hours after being born. Giraffes run in an unusual way. As their front legs push backward, their back legs swing forward outside the front ones. They run gracefully and as fast as 35 miles (56 kilometers) an hour.

Goat

(**goht**) The goat has been called the "poor man's cow" because it gives milk, but is easier to care for than a cow. Goats can survive where grass is scarce. They eat all sorts of plants. Goats stand tall on their hind legs, or even climb trees, in order to reach leaves and twigs. However, goats do not eat "tin" cans, as is commonly believed. They explore many objects with their sensitive lips, and may lick or chew on a metal object when they crave certain minerals in their diets.

Goats are sure-footed on steep hillsides and narrow trails. The play of young goats, called kids, is full of leaps and games of "king of the hill." Kids even leap on and off their mothers' backs. From an early age, goat kids also butt foreheads and push against one another. This process establishes which goats are leaders and which are followers in a herd. A pair of adult male goats, called bucks or billies, butt heads and wrestle with their horns in order to settle the issue of which buck is the boss.

On goat dairy farms, dozens of female goats, called does, produce milk that some people prefer to cows' milk. Certain breeds of goats, called cashmere and Angora, are also raised for their hair, which is clipped twice a year and made into fine cloth.

Goldfish

(**gohld**-fish) Many people have had just one brief experience in keeping a fish as a pet. They receive a goldfish in a small glass bowl, and the fish soon dies. Goldfish need more space. They often die from lack of oxygen, which enters the water from the air. A fish tank with more water surface receives more oxygen. Given proper care, a goldfish can live for ten years. Some have lived more than thirty years. They are not the most remarkable aquarium fish, but are easy to keep, and have some intelligence. When some goldfish were trained to open a little door to get food, other goldfish learned the trick simply by watching.

Common goldfish kept in garden pools or ponds may grow to weigh several pounds (kilograms). They resemble their ancient ancestors, wild goldfish (a kind of carp) that were raised for food in China centuries ago. By selecting certain goldfish for mating, people in China and Japan gradually produced many different varieties of aquarium goldfish. Today, there are more than one hundred to choose from. They vary in tail size, shape, and color. Some goldfish are multicolored; for example, blue mottled with red, brown, yellow, and black. Some are completely black. "Telescope" goldfish have entirely normal eyes until they are about two months old. Then the eyes bulge out in a "pop-eyed" look.

Gorilla

(guh-**ril**-uh) At the zoo, there is always a crowd of viewers at the gorilla display. People are fascinated by these huge but gentle apes, partly because they are fellow primates. Gorillas are related to chimpanzees, orangutans, and humans. They are the biggest primates. A male mountain gorilla often weighs more than 500 pounds (227 kilograms).

Wild gorillas live in Africa, and there are three varieties: the mountain gorilla, Eastern lowland gorilla, and Western lowland gorilla. All gorillas live in family groups, called troops, that are led by a large male, the silverback. The name comes from the silvery hair that grows on a male gorilla's back when it is about eleven years old.

The members of a troop of gorillas often sit down to eat, reaching out with long arms to select foods they like. They can climb high in trees to reach fruit. At the end of a day spent searching for fruit, seeds, and other plant food, the silverback chooses a resting place for the night. The members of the gorilla troop bend and break tree branches to create a platform or nest on which to sleep.

The number of gorillas in the wild has dropped sharply because they are sometimes killed, and because the dense forests they need to live in are being cut down. Their survival depends on people working together to save their forest habitat in Africa.

Grasshopper

(**gras**-hahp-uhr) The grasshopper is well named. It is often found in grassy fields and it takes large jumps. Its back legs are long and strong. Grasshoppers also have wings and can fly, but they usually move by walking and hopping among the plants they eat. Plenty of grasshoppers can be seen in meadows and other areas with low-growing plants, but they live in other habitats, too, including treeless mountaintops and deserts.

The color of a grasshopper usually matches its surroundings. A gray grasshopper is well hidden on the stony ground of a desert, and may escape notice by a predator. Spiders, birds, snakes, lizards, and many other animals hunt for grasshoppers. Two kinds of mice are so fond of eating grasshoppers that they are called grasshopper mice.

In summer, a chorus of grasshopper sounds rises from meadows and fields. Males make chirps, buzzes, and other sounds by rubbing one body part on another; for example, a leg against a wing. In the autumn, all adult grasshoppers usually die, but not until the females have laid eggs in the soil. A new generation of grasshoppers hatches from eggs in the spring. In some years, conditions are just right for huge numbers of young grasshoppers to survive. Millions of them look for food. They sometimes fly long distances. When the grasshoppers land, they eat farm crops and all other plants in their path. They are called a "plague of locusts," because the grasshopper species involved are sometimes called locusts.

Guinea Pig

(**gin**-ee pig) Small rodents called cavies live in some South American mountain ranges and grasslands. There are about twenty different species, but each kind eats seeds, grasses, and other plant foods. They live in family groups, and hide among rocks and in tall grass.

About four hundred years ago, some tame cavies were taken to Europe aboard sailing ships. People began to keep and breed cavies as pets, and to call them guinea pigs. No one is sure why they were given that name. Perhaps their squeaks reminded people of the sound of baby pigs. And perhaps the first cavies in England were each sold for a gold British coin that was called the guinea.

Today, guinea pigs are popular pets. They can live five years or longer. Like all rodents, guinea pigs have front teeth that grow throughout their lives. They need to gnaw on carrots or blocks of wood in order to wear away the tips of these teeth. Guinea pigs are only about 8 inches (20 centimeters) long, and cannot escape captivity easily because they do not climb or burrow. Like wild cavies, they are active in the day and sleep at night. Guinea pigs are timid but enjoy gentle grooming and cuddling.

Gull

(**guhl**) When you imagine an ocean beach, you probably think of two sounds: waves crashing on the shore and the cries of a gull. There are forty-three different species of gulls, including the herring gull, laughing gull, and western gull (shown here), but none called the seagull. Some gulls live far from the sea; for example, along the shores of the Great Lakes or Great Salt Lake in Utah.

Wherever gulls are, they eat a great variety of food, dead and alive. To get at the animal inside a clamshell, gulls sometimes carry the clam into the air, then drop it onto rocks, a road, or even the top of a car, cracking the shell open. Gulls are extraordinary fliers. They make good use of uprising air along shores. They soar and glide, scouting for food without using much energy.

Guppy

(**guhp**-ee) Wild guppies are small fish that live in ponds, lakes, and slow-flowing streams of the tropics. When fully grown, they are only about 1½ inches (4 centimeters) long. Guppies are named after a British scientist, Dr. Robert Guppy, who was among the first to collect and study them. Wild guppies are usually a brownish-gray color. However,

by allowing guppies with different characteristics to mate, aquarium keepers have produced many colorful varieties. Some have unusual tails and are called veiltails, delta tails, and swordtails. Guppies are hardy, easy to care for, and one of the most popular of all aquarium fishes.

Hamster

(**ham**-stuhr) Wild hamsters live in underground burrows. They sleep in a snug nest chamber in the daytime. At night, they hunt for seeds and other plant foods. After a hamster stuffs its cheek pouches full of seeds, it carries this food back to a storage chamber in its burrow. Hamster cheek pouches are stretchy. They hold a surprising amount of seeds. A hamster can stuff seeds into its cheek pouches that equal about one-half of its body weight. This hoarding of food led to the hamster's name. In German, the word *hamstern* means "to hoard."

Tame hamsters may also hoard food in their cages. They are solitary creatures, and fights break out if two hamsters are kept in the same cage. However, with their gentle ways and appealing big black eyes, hamsters are popular pets. Nearly all of the varieties of hamsters available from pet stores today are descendants of rare golden hamsters captured in a Syrian desert in 1930. Other varieties of hamsters include the dwarf hamster of western Asia and the rabbit-sized common hamster of central Europe, which is aggressive and does not make a good pet.

Hamsters are rodents, related to mice, rats, and guinea pigs. Their big front teeth grow constantly, so they need to gnaw on a piece of wood or other hard object to keep their teeth sharp and at the proper length. Whether in the wild or in a cage, a hamster has a short life of about one thousand days. Hamsters rarely live longer than three years.

Hermit Crab

(**huhr**-mit krab) In many ways, a hermit crab is like other crabs. It is a crustacean with five pairs of jointed legs. It uses most of its legs for walking, but the first pair is claws, used to grab and hold things. And, like most crabs, the hermit crab's eyes are on stalks that can move in different directions.

The hermit crab also has a hard outer covering on its body, called an exoskeleton. However, the back section of its body, the abdomen, has no protective exoskeleton. Its abdomen is unusually long and soft, and would be a tasty meal for a predator. The hermit crab protects itself by sticking its soft abdomen inside an empty shell that once belonged to a whelk, periwinkle, or other marine snail. The hermit's abdomen is curved and fits perfectly inside a spiral-shaped shell. The crab holds onto the inside of the shell with its rear legs.

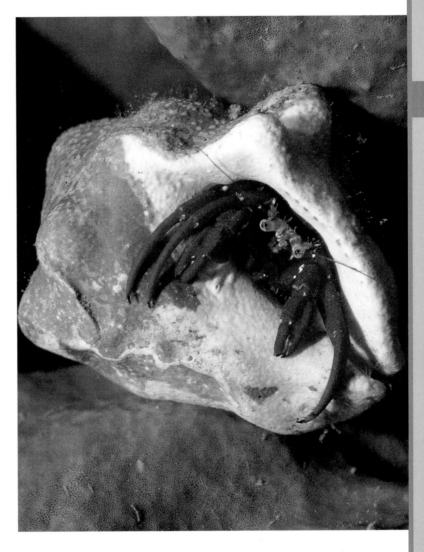

Hauling its borrowed shell along, the crab goes about its normal life, walking about and eating both plants and animals, dead or alive. However, there are times when it must leave its protective shell to mate or to move into a larger shell. All crabs grow by shedding their old exoskeleton and emerging with a new, bigger one. This process is called molting. Soon after a hermit crab molts, it must find a larger shell to live in. When it finds one the right size, the hermit crab cleans out pebbles and sand, then quickly pulls its abdomen out of its old shell and snuggles into the new one.

Hippopotamus

(hip-uh-**paht**-uh-muhs) The name hippopotamus comes from two Greek words that mean "river horse." Although hippos are not related to horses, the "river" part of their name is apt because they spend so much of their lives in the shallow water of slow-flowing rivers. The hippo's name was actually given first to the common hippopotamus that lives in Central and East Africa. The much smaller pygmy hippo survives in small numbers in West Africa. It is about the size of a large pig, and weighs no more than 500 pounds (227 kilograms). In contrast, a common hippo can weigh as much as 8,000 pounds (3,629 kilograms). Its head alone may weigh ½ ton (0.5 tonne).

The common hippo is Earth's third-largest land animal (after the rhinoceros and elephant). It is a plant-eating giant, though it has huge, sharp teeth at the front of its jaws. When a male hippo opens its mouth wide, showing those teeth, it is not yawning. It is giving a warning. Hippos sometimes kill lions and crocodiles, and a battle between two male hippos sometimes ends in death for one.

Hippos come ashore in the evening and eat grass most of the night. In the daytime, water is their safe resting place. The eyes, ears, and nostrils of the common hippo are on top of its head, so it can be almost completely underwater, yet still see, hear, and smell.

Horse

(**hors**) The energy output of automobile engines is measured in horsepower—a reminder that horses once did work that is now done by machines. However, horses are still at work all over the world. They pull plows and wagons on some farms, including those of Amish and Mennonite people in the United States. Horses help herd cattle on ranches, and help police control crowds and traffic in cities. Millions of horses are ridden for fun. The palomino and the quarter horse (shown here) are two breeds used for riding. Other breeds that are used to pull heavy loads, called draft horses, include the Clydesdale and Percheron.

A horse's body and senses are well suited for a life on open, grassy plains. A horse has large eyes and flexible ears that help it watch and listen for enemies. Its hooves, legs, and powerful shoulder muscles allow it to flee quickly, or travel at a slow but steady pace for many miles (kilometers). With its long neck, the horse easily reaches down to graze on short grasses. It uses its lips and front teeth to grab and cut grass. Then its tongue pushes the grass to the back of its mouth, where sharp ridges on the top of its cheek teeth grind the grass into little bits. Given a chance, most tame horses can thrive in the wild, as their ancestors did thousands of years ago.

Hummingbird

(**huhm**-ing-buhrd) Some birds are named for their songs, but hummingbirds are named for the swift whirring sound of their wings. The wings beat, on average, seventy-eight times a second, and even faster when a hummingbird dives. Hummingbirds can hover in one place, fly backward or to either side, and fly upside down. They burn a lot of energy, so they must eat frequently. Hummingbirds fly from flower to flower— bright red is their favorite color—sticking

their long beaks deep into the blossom and lapping up sweet nectar with their long tongues. More than three hundred species of hummingbirds live in the Americas, with sixteen in the United States, including the black-chinned hummingbird (shown here) in the Southwest.

Hyena

(hie-**ee**-nuh) Hyenas are famous for their sounds. The spotted hyena is one of the noisiest animals of Africa. At night, hyenas can produce a chorus of scary sounds, including moans, whoops, and crazy laughs.

Female hyenas are bigger than males and are the leaders of groups, called **clans**, that hunt together. Each clan has a territory and defends its borders against neighboring clans. A hyena mother usually gives birth to

twin pups, and hides them in a small burrow where large animals can't reach them. The pups come to the burrow entrance to nurse milk from their mother. Long after they are big enough to leave the den, their mother must protect them from being eaten by lions or even by older male hyenas.

Iguana

(i-**gwahn**-uh) The iguana family of lizards totals about seven hundred different species that live in North, South, and Central America and on nearby islands. Iguanas live in all sorts of habitats, including forests, deserts, and seashores. They differ in many ways, but all iguanas have scaly bodies and five toes on each foot, tipped with long, sharp claws. Many iguanas have a ridge, or crest, running along their backs and tails. The green iguana (shown here) is often kept as a pet.

An iguana's tail makes up one-half or more of its total length. Its tail helps the iguana keep its balance when it is moving fast on the ground. Its tail also makes the iguana a strong swimmer. Some iguanas drop from trees into water and swim away to escape an enemy. The most remarkable swimming iguana is the marine iguana of the Galápagos Islands, west of Ecuador. It dives into chilly ocean water—not to escape, but to eat seaweed and algae that grow underwater. Then it crawls out onto rocks and warms its body in the sun.

Most iguanas are plant eaters, though they may catch insects when they are young. Some iguanas called horned lizards eat ants all of their lives. They often hide near ant nests and quickly snap up any ant that comes near.

Jellyfish

(**jel**-ee-fish) The name "jellyfish" comes from the soft, swishy bodies of these animals. Jellyfish have no bones, but they do have muscles, a mouth, and tentacles that enable them to catch food and defend themselves. Jellyfish can be found in every ocean on Earth. They are most abundant in the tropics, but also live in the frigid waters around Antarctica. The moon jelly (shown here) lives in the Arctic Ocean.

A jellyfish's body is called a bell. It is often shaped like a bell or an umbrella. A jellyfish swims by letting water into its bell, then squeezing its muscles, forcing some water out. As the water rushes out, the jellyfish is pushed along.

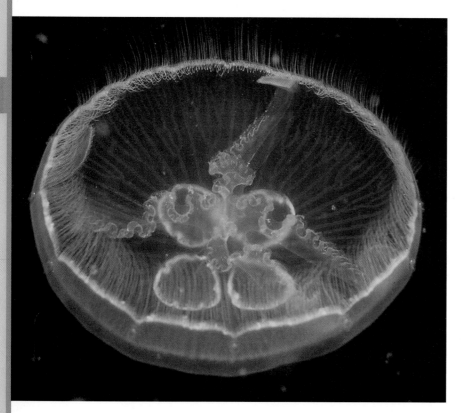

Tentacles dangle beneath the bell. This moon jelly has short tentacles, but the tentacles of other kinds of jellyfish can be several feet (meters) long. A jellyfish species that lives far beneath the surface off the coast of California has tentacles up to 130 feet (39 meters) in length—longer than a blue whale. Another species floats upside down near the sea bottom, with its tentacles reaching upward in the water.

Jellyfish tentacles are covered with stinging cells that can stun or kill fish, shrimp, or other small animals that swim too close. They become food for a jellyfish. Jellyfish are protected from many predators by their stinging tentacles, although ocean sunfish and sea turtles eat jellyfish without being harmed. The sting of most jellyfish causes only a skin rash on humans, but one species has a deadly sting—the sea wasp jellyfish, which lives near Australia.

Kangaroo

(kang-guh-**roo**) Toads hop and sparrows hop, but only one kind of big mammal hops—the kangaroo. It has large back feet and long, strong leg muscles. One-half of a kangaroo's total weight is muscle. Sometimes a male kangaroo uses its powerful back legs in battle with another male. A kangaroo can jump in the air and lash out with both back feet at once.

Large kangaroos can leap over a 10-foot-(3-meter) tall fence, and zoom along in a graceful hop at 40 miles (64 kilometers) an hour—faster than a racehorse. That is how most people picture kangaroos, bounding over the open grassland. However, about sixty different kinds of kangaroos live in Australia and nearby islands. Some climb in forest trees. Some, called rock wallabies, leap about on cliffs.

Large or small, all kangaroos eat plants, and all are **marsupials**. This means that a tiny young kangaroo, right after being born, crawls into a pouch on its mother's belly. The baby, called a joey, nurses milk from its mother. The joey develops for about nine months within the pouch before it is able to venture out—and hop—on its own. The joey begins to eat grass, but continues to nurse milk from its mother until it is one year old.

Koala

(koh-**ahl**-uh) A koala's face and its furry body remind many people of a bear. But a koala is not a bear. It is a marsupial. Kangaroos and opossums are also marsupials.

When a tiny, naked koala is born, it crawls to a pouch on its mother's belly. Within the pouch, it finds a nipple and begins to nurse milk. A baby koala stays safely in its mother's pouch, feeding and growing, for about six months. Then its eyes open and it is ready to explore the outside world. A young koala often rides piggyback on its mother before it begins to scamper about in trees by itself. Koalas eat the leaves of certain eucalyptus, or gum trees, in the forests of eastern Australia.

Ladybug

(**layd**-ee-buhg) "Bug" is a common name for all insects, but most are not true bugs. The ladybug is a beetle. Nearly five hundred species of ladybugs live in North America, and nearly every kind is a predator of other insects. Both adult and larval ladybugs feed on mites, aphids, and other soft-bodied insects. They are appreciated by gardeners, farmers, and foresters because they eat so many plant pests. A single ladybug larva can eat three hundred aphids in two weeks.

Ladybugs can fly, but their wings are usually hidden by brightly colored wing covers. In the autumn, they cluster by the thousands under tree bark, inside houses, and in other dry, cool shelters for the winter.

Leopard

(**lep**-uhrd) Wild leopards are often photographed in trees. Leopards are excellent climbers, and frequently sleep and eat in trees. Sometimes a leopard's ability to climb saves its life when it flees from lions or hyenas. Leopards are big, powerful cats, sometimes weighing 160 pounds (73 kilograms), but are smaller than lions. They hunt at night. They eat gazelles, impalas, baboons, and many other mammals, as well as birds, snakes, and even insects. When a leopard kills a large animal, it often drags the body to a tree and pulls it up onto a limb to keep it from other predators.

Leopards live alone for most of their lives, which may last fifteen years in the wild. A male and female spend a few days together when they mate, then the male leaves. About three months later, the female gives birth to a litter of one to four cubs. Leopard mothers take good care of their young, but cubs may be killed by eagles, lions, hyenas, or even male leopards. Often only one cub from a litter survives to become an adult.

Leopards live in a variety of habitats, including jungles and deserts, in Africa and Asia. Each leopard has a pattern of spots on its face and body that is like no other. Some jungle leopards are pure black, and are called black panthers.

Lion

(**lie**-uhn) In many ways, a lion is like all other cats. Lions sleep a lot, sometimes twenty hours a day. Lions can run fast—up to 35 miles (56 kilometers) an hour—but only for short distances. In other ways, however, lions are unusual cats. Only tigers in Asia are bigger. Lions may reach 500 pounds (227 kilograms) in weight and 11 feet (3.4 meters) in length. Part of that length is an unusual tail that is tipped with a tuft of black hair. Lions are also the only kind of cat in which the males have a shaggy mane. And lions can roar but they cannot purr.

Most remarkable is the social life of lions. They live in family groups called prides. A pride usually includes several males, more females, and their young, which are called cubs. Each pride has a territory that the lions defend against other lions that might intrude. The roar of a lion can be heard from 5 miles (8 kilometers) away, and it is one way in which it defends its territory. Sometimes a male lion dies in a battle defending the territory of its pride.

Members of a lion pride often hunt as a team. The females, called lionesses, do most of the hunting. One lioness may chase an antelope or other prey in a direction where other lionesses are waiting in ambush. Once an animal is killed, the lions eat first, then the lionesses, then the cubs.

A B C D E F G H I J K **L** M N O P Q R S T U V W X Y Z

Lizard

(**liz**-uhrd) Lizards can be small enough to fit in your hand or as long as a car. Nearly four thousand kinds of lizards live on Earth. They include iguanas, chameleons, geckos, swifts, skinks, chuckwallas, horned lizards, and fence lizards (shown here). A lizard that looks like the horned lizards of North America lives in the deserts of Australia. It is a harmless, small lizard that eats ants but has a scary name: the thorny devil. Another lizard that sounds dangerous is the Gila monster of North American deserts. It has a poisonous bite, but moves slowly and avoids people.

Among the many amazing lizards on Earth are those that have flaps of skin along their sides that enable them to glide from tree to tree. One is called the flying dragon. The basilisk lizard of Central America can rear up on its back legs and run across water. Its great speed and big feet keep it from sinking.

Nearly all lizards have tails as long as their bodies. Some are plant eaters, but most catch insects and other live food. One of the world's biggest lizards, the Komodo dragon, is able to kill and eat pigs, deer, and occasionally, a person.

Llama

(**lahm**-uh) There were no horses or camels in the mountains of South America, so people needed a big animal to carry heavy loads. They tamed wild guanacos and, after many years of selective breeding, produced the llama, the largest of a group of mammals called lamoids. Other lamoids are the alpaca, vicuña, and guanaco. Llamas can weigh 400 pounds (181 kilograms) and stand 5 feet (1.5 meters) tall at the shoulder. They proved to be valuable pack animals, as well as a source of food and wool. Today, llamas are kept as pets in every one of the United States, and can sometimes be seen on wilderness trails carrying tents and other camping gear. Llamas are gentle creatures, but have the ability to spit when scared or annoyed. A llama can spit saliva from its mouth or a foul-smelling fluid from its stomach. Llamas have good aim, but usually spit at other llamas, not at people.

Lobster

(**lahb**-stuhr) Most people see lobsters only in restaurants. They see the big-clawed American lobster or the spiny lobster (shown here). But a lobster is much more than an expensive item on a menu. It is an animal with remarkable senses that can live more than fifty years.

At night, a lobster emerges from its ocean hideout and begins to hunt for food. It can't see very well, but learns a lot about its surroundings with two different kinds of antennae. Its long antennae have a keen sense of

touch. Delicate hairs on its short antennae are able to identify more than four hundred different scents. A lobster's body and legs are also covered with tiny hairs that detect smells and tastes in the water. A lobster's keen senses help it find both food and a mate on the dark ocean floor.

Manatee

(**man**-uh-tee) When a baby manatee is born, it somehow knows that it must paddle up to the water's surface to take its first breath of air. A manatee is a mammal, not a fish. An adult manatee can stay underwater for about four minutes, but then needs to breathe.

Manatees are big, slow-moving plant eaters, sometimes called sea cows. They are bulky, but are graceful swimmers. One kind of manatee lives in the freshwater of South America's Amazon River. Two other kinds of manatees can live in both salt water and freshwater. One is found along the coast of West Africa. The other lives in parts of North and South America, including the rivers and bays of Florida and other southeastern states. Manatees also have a relative, the dugong, that feeds on plants along the coasts of East Africa, Asia, New Guinea, and Australia.

A fully grown manatee often measures 12 feet (3.7 meters) long and weighs about 1 ton (0.9 tonne). Most of its weight is stored fat. The fat helps keep the manatee warm. The fat is also a supply of food that helps the manatee survive when plants are scarce. Manatees are killed or injured when hit by speedboats, and can die when water becomes polluted. The numbers of these harmless, gentle giants have dropped very low.

Millipede

(**mil**-uh-peed) A millipede's body looks like the hose of a vacuum cleaner—with legs. Its long, round body is made up of many segments, with two pairs of legs on each segment. The name "millipede" means "thousand legs." However, none of the eight thousand species of millipedes on Earth has more than three hundred legs. A millipede in motion is a beautiful sight as it seems to flow along the ground. Groups of legs step together, creating a wavelike movement.

Some kinds of millipedes measure 12 inches (30 centimeters) long but most are much smaller. One tiny species is only ⅛ inch (3 millimeters) long. Day or night, you can often find millipedes ambling along among decaying leaves in gardens or forests. Most millipedes munch on dead leaves that

have begun to decay. Some eat seeds and mushrooms. Some millipedes can be garden pests because they eat live leaves and seedlings.

A bird or lizard that tries to eat a millipede may get an unpleasant surprise. Most millipedes have two rows of stink glands along the sides of their bodies. The glands give out a bad-smelling and bitter-tasting fluid when a millipede is in danger. This usually causes the bird or other predator to drop the millipede. A millipede also defends itself by coiling its body into a tight spiral. Its head is always in the safest place, in the center of the coil.

One species of millipede is able to produce a poison gas that kills ants or other small creatures that come too close. The amount of gas is too small to harm humans. Unlike centipedes, millipedes do not bite. In the daytime, millipedes can sometimes be found resting beneath stones or pieces of wood.

Monkey

(**muhng**-kee) People love to watch monkeys at the zoo. The monkeys leap from limb to limb in trees. They clean one another's fur. The looks on their faces and the ways in which they use their hands cause people to say, "They're almost human." People and monkeys are alike in many ways. They are part of a large group of mammals called primates. Most primates have thumbs or big toes that stick out to the side which can touch the fingers or the other toes of that hand or foot. Humans use their thumbs to grasp things. Some monkeys can grab or pick up things equally well with either their hands or feet.

Many of the monkeys that live in Central and South America, called New World monkeys, are also able to grip vines or branches with their tails. The white-faced monkey (shown here) lives in Costa Rica, so it is a New World monkey. Others include squirrel, spider, woolly, capuchin, tamarin, and howler monkeys. Howler monkeys are famous for their loud calls that can be heard for several miles (kilometers).

Old World monkeys include macaque, colobus, guenon, and langur monkeys as well as baboons and mandrills. They live in Asia or Africa.

Moose

(**moos**) The Algonquin Indians had a name for the huge, dark forest animals that fed on trees and shrubs. They called them "moose," which means "twig eater." (In northern Europe, moose are called elk.) A full-grown bull moose often weighs more than 1,000 pounds (454 kilograms), so it has a big appetite. It sometimes eats 50 pounds (23 kilograms) of twigs and leaves a day. With its long legs, a moose can easily reach twigs and leaves that are between 4 and 10 feet (1.2 and 3 meters) off the ground. Sometimes a moose uses its body to bend a sapling close to the ground so it can reach the tree's upper branches. If a moose wants to eat low-growing plants, it must kneel down to reach them.

In the summertime, moose wade and swim in lakes and ponds, eating water plants and keeping cool. Even though moose have spread southward in New England and other northern states, they thrive in cold weather. A winter night with below-zero temperatures is comfortable for a moose with its double-layered hair coat.

Summer is antler-growing season for bull moose. By September, the antlers have reached their full size—rather small on a young bull, massive on an older bull. A bull moose's antlers can measure 6 feet (1.8 meters) across and weigh 75 pounds (34 kilograms).

Mosquito

(muh-**skeet**-oh) One of the most annoying sounds in nature is the whine of a mosquito as it closes in, aiming to take blood from you. The sound comes from its wings, which beat at a rate of three hundred times a second. If it can, the mosquito will pierce your skin with sharp mouthparts called stylets. Another part then sucks blood up into the mosquito's abdomen. Only female mosquitoes do this. They need protein from blood to nourish their eggs, which they lay in ponds, puddles, and other places with still water. Some mosquito species often lay their eggs in the water that collects in abandoned tires. There are 3,500 kinds of mosquitoes worldwide and 150 species in the United States. Most species are annoying but harmless. A few kinds of mosquitoes carry malaria or other diseases.

Moth

(**mawth**) As darkness falls, moths take wing. You may see them fluttering against the glass of a window, or whirling around an outdoor lightbulb. In the daytime, moths rest with their wings spread flat, unlike most butterflies, which rest with their wings held above their bodies. Most kinds of moths have four small eyes on their heads, but the Io moth (shown here) seems to have huge eyes on its wings. These big eye spots are not real eyes, but may scare away birds that eat moths.

Moth larvae are called caterpillars. They include inchworms and woolly bear caterpillars. The caterpillars spin a silken shelter called a **cocoon**. After many changes within its cocoon, an adult moth emerges and flies into the night.

Mouse (**mous**) The word *mouse* brings many images to mind: pests that may carry disease; laboratory mice that are used in research that helps human health; or that lovable cartoon mouse, Mickey. Although all mice are small rodents, related to squirrels, rats, and beavers, they are a large and varied group. Most people see mice only in pet stores, or see house mice that sneak into buildings and are considered pests. Many other kinds of mice live outdoors, in deserts, jungles, salt marshes, and the Arctic. These mice play important roles in nature, eating weed seeds and other plant food, and being eaten by owls, foxes, and other predators.

One of the most abundant mouse species in North America is the meadow vole. (Voles are short-tailed, small-eared mice, and are not the same as moles, which burrow underground and are not rodents.) One female meadow vole can have as many as seventeen litters of four to nine babies in a year. Other common mice include deer mice, usually found in forests. Their big eyes and ears, plus the color of their fur, remind people of deer. They sing, sometimes making a high-pitched trill or buzzing sound in the night. Like most mice, deer mice eat fruit and seeds. However, a few species of mice are predators. Grasshopper mice attack and eat insects, spiders, scorpions, and even other kinds of mice.

Octopus

(**ahk**-tuh-puhs) People once believed an octopus was a huge undersea monster that attacked humans, but most kinds are small, and they are all gentle and shy. The biggest species is called the Pacific giant octopus. It can measure 12 feet (3.7 meters) across from the tip of one arm to the opposite tip.

An octopus has eight arms in all, each lined with two rows of muscular suckers. More than 1,200 suckers enable it to crawl, grip food, move rocks, and even help it to solve puzzles like unscrewing the lid of a jar containing food. Scientists have also watched an octopus in an aquarium find its way through a maze. Octopuses are related to clams and snails in a group called mollusks, but are no ordinary mollusks. They are probably as intelligent as cats or dogs.

In the wild, an octopus can swim, jet quickly through the water, or crawl along the sea bottom. It can hide from enemies or wait to grab some food by changing color to match its surroundings. An octopus can change from blue to orange in a few seconds. It can also release ink that makes a black underwater cloud. An ink cloud can help the octopus escape from a shark, or creep up on a lobster or crab the octopus wants to eat.

Opossum

(uh-**pahs**-uhm) Have you ever "played possum?" If you lie still with your eyes closed, trying to fool someone into believing that you are asleep or unconscious, you are "playing possum." Sometimes a real opossum does the same thing. Attacked by a dog or other enemy, an opossum may fall on its side with its mouth open. Its body goes limp. The opossum can be picked up, poked, and shaken but it shows no sign of life. Often the animal that attacked the opossum will then leave. A few minutes later, the opossum leaps to its feet and runs away.

The name *opossum* comes from a Native American word that means "white beast." The only opossum that lives in the United States and Canada (shown here) does have plenty of white fur, especially on its head. Many other kinds of opossums live in Central and South America. One is as small as a mouse. Small or large, all opossums are marsupials. Right after being born, baby opossums crawl into a pouch on their mother's belly. There each baby puts its mouth around a nipple and holds tight, nursing milk and growing for more than two months. When they are big enough to leave the pouch, they often cling to their mother's fur and ride along as she hunts for food. Young opossums can hang by their tails from a tree limb. Older opossums, as big as house cats, are too heavy to do this, but can grab limbs with their tails as they climb.

Orangutan

(uh-**rang**-uh-tan) The name *orangutan* means "person of the forest" in the Malay language of Indonesia. Long ago, the Malay people chose this name because orangutans look and act so human. Adult male orangutans look like hairy old men, and they weigh about as much as a human male. Like humans, orangutans are primates. They are related to gorillas and chimpanzees.

Orangutans are gentle and intelligent. They use simple tools; for example, choosing sticks of the right size to scratch their backs. They have also been observed using sticks to break through the tough skin of fruit they like to eat. Orangutans gather most of their food among the treetops—the **canopy**—in tropical rain forests. Their exceptionally long arms enable orangutans to reach out and grab branches and move gracefully through the treetops. They walk slowly and awkwardly on land, but are seldom there.

All through the year, orangutans find fruit, flowers, nuts, leaves, and insects to eat high overhead in rain forests that remain on the islands of Borneo and Sumatra. As long as this special habitat is not destroyed, orangutans will continue to live in the wild.

Ostrich

(**ahs**-trich) The ostrich is the largest bird in the world. It is much bigger than condors or eagles, and bigger than its close relatives—emus, rheas, and cassowaries, which are all flightless birds. A male ostrich stands 8 feet (2.4 meters) tall and can weigh more than 400 pounds (181 kilograms).

Ostriches have long necks and long, powerful legs. An ostrich never spreads its small wings for flight, but sometimes holds them out to help keep balance as it races across the plains of Africa. It zooms along at more

than 40 miles (64 kilometers) an hour —faster than a horse. An ostrich usually runs from trouble, but can kick with great power and sharp toenails when defending its eggs. (Ostrich eggs weigh 3 pounds [1.4 kilograms] and are the biggest of all bird eggs.)

Flocks of ostriches graze on plants, often traveling with herds of zebras and antelopes. With their height and keen vision, ostriches are good at spotting a lion or other predator. They also reach down to grab insects, small lizards, and snakes.

You may have heard people say, "Don't be an ostrich and stick your head in the sand," a saying that means "don't ignore problems" or "face the truth." No one knows the origins of this expression. Perhaps someone saw ostrichs put their heads down to tend their eggs, which are in shallow nests in the sand. The ostrich *never* bends down and actually sticks its head in the sand.

Otter

(**aht**-uhr) Most of the otters on Earth live in freshwater rivers and lakes, and are called river otters. They include the giant otter of Brazil, which grows to be 7 feet (2.1 meters) long. River otters are known for their playfulness. Whether young or adult, they dive and play chasing games in the water, and slide down slopes of mud or snow.

Sea otters (shown here) live along coasts of the North Pacific Ocean. They rarely come ashore. Sea otters eat and sleep while lying on their backs in the water. Their lungs are unusually large, enabling them to dive deep and gather clams, sea urchins, and other food. To open a clam, an otter smacks it against a stone it balances on its chest. When the otter finishes a meal, it clears away the stone and bits of shell from its body by simply rolling over in the water.

Unlike seals and whales, sea otters do not have a layer of fat to protect them in cold waters, so they spend several hours a day grooming their fur. They roll and twist in the water, reaching every bit of fur. Sea otters have the thickest hair of all mammals. By spreading natural oils from their skin on it, and by combing it with their claws and blowing into it, sea otters allow air bubbles to be trapped deep in their fur. This protects them from the chilly ocean water.

Owl (owl) Film directors often use the call of an owl to help create a scary mood for a night scene. In the dark, the low hoot of an owl can send a shiver down your spine. But owls never hurt people, and their hoots and other sounds are their way of communicating with other owls. About three hundred kinds of owls live on Earth and they make a great variety of sounds, including coos, whinnies, and wails. The screech owl of Europe does screech, but a different owl of the same name in North America gives a soft, warbling whinny.

Most owls are **nocturnal**—they sleep in the day and hunt at night. Their big eyes work well in dim light. Owls also have extraordinary hearing. Many owls, including the great horned owl (shown here), have feathers that look like ears sticking up on the top of their head. Their real ears are openings at the sides of their head, hidden by feathers. Perched on a branch, an owl looks and listens for a mouse on the move—in leaves or even under snow. The owl has fourteen neck bones, twice as many as humans, and can turn its head until it is almost facing backward. When a mouse is detected, the owl's soft-edged feathers allow it to swoop down silently on its prey. The mouse is caught in the owl's sharp claws, or talons.

Panda

(**pan**-duh) In the misty mountain forests of central China lives one of the world's most beloved animals, the giant panda. Only a few hundred remain in the bamboo forests that are vital to the panda's survival. The giant panda eats bamboo. The giant panda has its favorites—about twenty of the three hundred different kinds of bamboo that grow in China. Its favorites grow high in the mountains, and the giant panda sometimes walks on top of deep snow as it searches for food. It eats stems, leaves, and fresh young shoots of bamboo, sometimes consuming more than 60 pounds (27 kilograms) a day. Giant pandas themselves can grow to weigh almost 300 pounds (136 kilograms) and stand 6 feet (1.8 meters) tall.

Pandas are related to bears, but differ from bears in several ways. A giant panda can take a firm grip on a piece of bamboo because of an unusual "thumb" on each of its front paws. The "thumb" is actually a wrist bone. Thanks to these "thumbs," pandas can hold food as tightly as a monkey or a person can. Giant pandas spend up to sixteen hours a day eating.

Giant pandas are gentle, shy creatures that are threatened with extinction. Adult pandas survive in zoos, but don't often produce young in them. If pandas are going to win the fight against **extinction**, people must protect all the pandas that remain, and their wild mountain habitat.

Panther (**pan**-thur)

"Panther" is just one name for this large wild cat that can weigh 200 pounds (91 kilograms) and measure 9 feet (2.7 meters) long. Its range stretches from northern Canada to the southern tip of South America. People in different regions gave it different names, including mountain lion, puma, cougar, and panther. Of these names, the oldest is puma, given to this big cat by the Inca people of South America. In Florida, these big cats are called panthers. Fewer than fifty panthers are left in southern Florida. Survival of the Florida panther depends on halting the destruction of the wild forest and swamp habitat it needs.

The numbers of some other populations of this big cat are growing. Sometimes a cougar or puma (as they are commonly called in the West) attacks a person hiking or jogging alone in a park or other wild area. Cougars are masters at sneaking up on prey, but they rarely harm people. They usually eat deer, moose, elk, rabbits, ground squirrels, and porcupines. Close to cities, they sometimes kill dogs and cats. Cougars hunt alone. They are great leapers, able to jump 15 feet (4.5 meters) in the air to reach a tree limb.

In one night, a cougar may travel as far as 25 miles (40 kilometers) as it hunts. These big, graceful cats also travel far in search of mates. Females mate just once every two years, and usually give birth to two or three cubs.

Parrot

(par-uht) Few people are lucky enough to see a flock of parrots flying in a tropical rain forest. With their large size and brilliant colors, it is a spectacular sight. Most people see parrots in a home or a pet shop, far from their natural habitat. Parrots are fascinating yet demanding pets. Large parrots, such as the blue-and-yellow macaw (shown here), can live as long as sixty years. They have loud voices and a lot to say: shrieks, squawks, whistles, and human words and other sounds they choose to mimic. Their beaks are powerful enough to break a wooden stick, but nimble enough to perform such delicate tasks as picking a tiny seed from its shell. Smaller parrots are more practical pets for most people. These include parakeets and cockatiels.

Peacock

(pee-kahk) It is courting time among the peafowl (shown here), and the peacock (male) spreads a spectacular display of feathers for the peahen (female). A peacock's fan of colorful feathers is called a train, and is separate from its tail feathers. A train is often more than 7 feet (2.1 meters) wide. The male gives the feathers a shivering motion, making the colors and eyespots more attractive. She may ignore him. If she pecks at the ground, however, it is a signal that she is interested in the peacock as a mate.

Peafowl are related to pheasants and quail. They still live wild in India, but for four thousand years they have been kept as tame birds in city parks and zoos.

Pelican

(**pel**-i-kuhn) In San Francisco Bay, Spanish explorers named an island Alcatraz, which means "pelican." For many years, Alcatraz was the site of a famous prison, and some of its inmates must have looked with envy at the free flight of pelicans. The pelican looks awkward on land, but the instant it faces the wind and lifts into the air, it becomes one of the most graceful and powerful of all fliers.

There are seven species of pelicans on Earth, including the white and brown pelicans of North America. Only the brown pelican (shown here) lives along coasts and hunts for fish in salt water. The white pelican fishes in large lakes of western Canada and the United States, and catches its prey while swimming.

A brown pelican glides along about 10 to 30 feet (3 to 9 meters) above the water, looking for fish near the surface. It folds its wings in a V shape and dives. As its beak pierces the water the bird thrusts its wings and legs backward, and slices into the water like an arrow. Sometimes a pelican stuns fish with the impact of its body hitting the water. Once underwater, the pelican opens its beak, and the pouch that is folded under the lower half stretches wide, forming a basket. When a fish is caught, the pelican swims to the surface. Water drains out of its pouch and the pelican tosses its head back, swallowing its catch. Catching fish this way takes great skill, and some young brown pelicans starve before they learn to do it well.

Penguin

(**pen**-gwin) In the southern half of the world, in some of Earth's coldest places, live seventeen kinds of birds that cannot fly—penguins. Dressed in black-and-white feathers and walking with a waddling gait, they are among the most appealing of all birds. They are slow-moving on land but strong, graceful swimmers. Penguins move through the water with their flippers, and steer with their feet and tail.

Swimming fast and darting through the water can save a penguin's life when it is chased by a leopard seal or a killer whale.

Emperor penguins (shown here) can dive more than 1,000 feet (304.8 meters) beneath the surface to catch small fish and crustaceans. They are the biggest penguins, standing 4 feet (1.2 meters) tall, and live on the ice that surrounds Antarctica. After a mother emperor penguin lays an egg, the male keeps it warm on the top of his feet while she walks many miles (kilometers) to the nearest open water to find food. Thousands of male penguins huddle together, trying to keep themselves and the eggs warm. They have nothing to eat and lose lots of weight. After about sixty-five days, the eggs hatch and the mothers return carrying food in their bellies that they spit up for their chicks. Then the mothers keep their chicks warm while the fathers go for food. Chicks have downy gray feathers at first, and cannot swim until they grow a coat of black-and-white waterproof feathers.

Pig

(**pig**) Whether you call them pigs, hogs, or swine, these animals are probably the smartest livestock on farms. Pigs have good memories and can be taught tricks. Growing numbers of families keep pigs as pets. However, since many varieties of pigs grow to weigh 200 pounds (91 kilograms) or more, the small Vietnamese potbellied pig is usually chosen to live in homes. It stands only 14 inches (36 centimeters) tall and weighs about 40 pounds (18 kilograms).

Pigs are very clean animals, though in hot weather, they wallow in mud in order to keep cool. They often get their noses dirty, too, poking their snouts underground in search of food. A pig's snout is both a tool for digging and a sensitive smelling organ. Pigs dig for roots, bulbs, insects, and worms. They can be trained to locate truffles—a highly valued mushroom that grows underground.

Millions of pigs are born and raised simply to provide food, including ham, pork, and bacon. Their skin is used to make gloves and other leather products. Pigs that have escaped from farms in warm climates have thrived and are called wild boars. In the southeastern United States, the wild boars are usually called razorbacks. The smart and appealing varieties of pigs that people see at agricultural fairs also have other wild relatives in Africa, including warthogs and giant forest hogs.

Pigeon (**pij**-uhn)

People usually ignore pigeons—those birds that walk with a jerky motion, pecking at crumbs on city sidewalks. Pigeons, however, are smart, fascinating birds. Thousands of years ago, their ancestors were rock doves that nested on ledges of cliffs in Europe and the Middle East. Rock doves ate mostly seeds, so they began to live near farms and villages, eat-

ing grains and nesting on buildings instead of cliffs. People tamed them, raising them for food or as pets. Some of these pigeons, as they were called, escaped or were let go in North America. Today, millions of pigeons live in cities and suburbs, and on farms. They find food on streets and in parks and vacant lots. They rest and nest on buildings and under bridges—places like the cliffs where rock doves lived long ago.

Tests in laboratories have shown that pigeons have a good memory. They can solve tough puzzles and learn to do tricks by simply watching other pigeons perform. They also have an amazing ability to find their way home when let go hundreds of miles (kilometers) away. Today, people raise a special breed of pigeon, the racing homer, and compete to see which bird returns home in the shortest time. Pigeons have been used in wartime to carry little containers holding messages to and from battlefields. Thousands of pigeons served in this way in World War II. They helped save many lives, and some received medals as animal heroes.

Piranha

(puh-**rahn**-uh) Piranhas have very sharp teeth shaped like triangles. South Americans have used the jaws taken from dead piranhas as cutting tools. They also use piranhas as a plentiful source of food, fishing for them in rivers, lakes, and ponds. But taking a fishhook out of a piranha's mouth is dangerous—a big piranha can easily snip off a fingertip. There are about thirty species of piranha in South America. Some eat mostly fruits and seeds; some nip off scales and parts of fins from other fish. A few big species, up to 2 feet (0.6 meter) long, eat fish and bigger prey. They are also scavengers, eating the flesh of dead animals. There is no proof that piranhas have ever attacked and killed a person. Every year, thousands of children and adults swim where piranhas live and are not harmed. However, people wisely avoid places where hungry piranhas are crowded together; for example, when they feed on an animal carcass in the water.

Plankton

(**plangk**-tuhn) Plankton are tiny animals and plants that live in salt water and freshwater, drifting or swimming near the surface. Many plankton organisms can be seen only with a microscope. Plant plankton has been called "the pasture of the sea," because all animal ocean life, from crabs to whales, depends on it. Some whales and some large sharks eat plankton directly. Other water animals depend on plankton indirectly; for example, by eating small fish or other creatures that depend on plankton for their food. The plants and animals that make

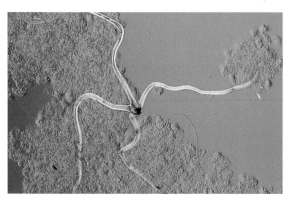

up plankton are the first links in many **food chains**. The most abundant plankton plants are called diatoms. Plankton animals include tiny crustaceans called copepods. The first small swimming stages in the life of clams, sea stars, crabs, and lobsters are also part of animal plankton.

Porcupine

(**por**-kyuh-pine) Porcupines are sometimes called "quill pigs," though they are not related to pigs at all. They are rodents, and are relatives of beavers, squirrels, and mice. Porcupines are also not related to the hedgehog, a small European mammal, but they share one characteristic with it: quills. The quills of a hedgehog are short and not very sharp. The quills of the American porcupine (shown here) are sometimes 3 inches (7.5 centimeters) long and are sharply pointed.

An adult American porcupine is armed with about thirty thousand of these weapons. Most of the time, the quills lie flat, hidden by long, dark hairs. When a dog or other enemy threatens, the quills rise up. The porcupine turns its back to the enemy and swings its tail back and forth. The tail is loaded with quills. Some are loosely attached and fly off as the tail swings. A dog standing too close can get a faceful of quills, and a painful lesson: Leave porcupines alone.

In the daytime, American porcupines sleep in a rocky den or hollow tree. At night, they amble about looking for forest plants to eat. They are good climbers, and sometimes eat and sleep overhead in trees, unnoticed. Sometimes people learn that a porcupine lives nearby when they discover that an axe handle or canoe paddle has been chewed. Sweaty hands leave traces of salt on such tools, and porcupines crave the taste of salt.

Prairie Dog

(**prair**-ee dawg) In 1804, explorers Lewis and Clark captured a prairie dog near present-day Nebraska. The caged prairie dog was carried by boat and wagon all the way to President Jefferson in Washington, D.C., where it lived in the president's house. Lewis and Clark came upon many large colonies, or towns, of these mammals, which they also called ground rats or barking squirrels. Prairie dogs are not dogs but are rodents, related to ground squirrels, and live only in the western grasslands of North America.

Prairie dogs must stay alert in their towns because coyotes, hawks, and golden eagles hunt them when they leave their burrows to feed on plants. Their grazing keeps grasses low, and sometimes they also nip off plant stems to have a clear view all around. At the sight of a hawk or other predator, a prairie dog gives a high-pitched bark. All of the prairie dogs in the town dash into their burrows.

Underground, prairie dogs have systems of tunnels and rooms. A nest room, about the size of a basketball, is lined with grass. Dried plants are stored in other, little rooms. Prairie dogs eat a lot before winter comes and become quite roly-poly with fat. All year long, prairie dog burrows provide shelter for many animals, including insects, mice, rabbits, and salamanders. Abandoned burrows are used as resting places by burrowing owls, and as homes by ground squirrels and black-footed ferrets.

Rabbit

(**rab**-it) Rabbits have big eyes, long ears, and strong back legs. They rarely walk: they hop and leap. Rabbits are not rodents, although they look somewhat like some rodents such as squirrels. The teeth of rodents and rabbits differ, and most rodents have long tails. Rabbits and their closest relatives, called hares, have short tails. In fact, the most common rabbits in North America have white fluffy tails that led to their name: cottontails.

The animals called jackrabbits and snowshoe rabbits are actually hares. They have longer ears and legs than rabbits. Also, baby hares are born with hair and with their eyes open. Within an hour of birth they can hop about. Baby rabbits are born naked, with eyes closed, and do not leave their nests until they are at least two weeks old.

Worldwide there are about forty species of rabbits and hares. Rabbits live in all sorts of habitats, including deserts, but most are found in fields or other places where there are plenty of low-growing plants. They eat only plants, and can be pests in gardens, orchards, and farmers' fields. Rabbits themselves can be farm animals, raised as a source of meat or fur, and tame rabbits of many colors are kept as pets. One of these is the lop-eared rabbit, whose ears may be 2 feet (0.6 meter) long.

Raccoon

(ra-**koon**) Say "raccoon" to some people and they think of words like "cute" and "clever." Others, however, think "masked marauder" and "pest." A native of North America, the raccoon has adapted very well to most of the changes made by people. It is more abundant today than it was when Europeans began to explore the Americas. It is an omnivore, eating both plant and animal food. Its diet includes nuts, berries, crayfish, frogs, earthworms—and pizza and whatever else it likes from human garbage. Not only is the raccoon adept at climbing, it can unlatch doors and break into garbage cans. People used to praise the raccoon for its cleanliness because it seems to wash its food. However, the raccoon simply has a basic need to grope underwater for food, which it sometimes satisfies by bringing a food item to the water's edge, then handling it underwater.

Rat

(**rat**) If someone calls you a rat, that person is probably not paying you a compliment. Many people do not know that rats have good qualities. They are intelligent, curious, and able to adapt to a wide variety of living situations. The varieties of rats that have been tamed make gentle pets. Rats are commonly used in medical research and drug testing, and information gained in such studies has saved countless human lives. To many people, however, the word *rat* means the black rat or the brown rat (sometimes called Norway rat) that are pests of homes and farms. They eat stored grain and other foods. These rats may spread diseases, because fleas that live on the rats sometimes pass along disease germs when they bite people.

Rhinoceros

(rie-**nahs**-uh-ruhs) The name rhinoceros comes from two Greek words that mean "nose" and "horn." All five species of rhinoceros have at least one horn. Three kinds of rhinos—the Indian, the Javan, and the Sumatran—live in Asia. The other two—the white and black rhinos—live in Africa and are the species people often see in zoos. Both kinds of African rhinos have two horns. The big front horn of a black rhino (shown here) blocks your view of a smaller horn behind it.

Both types of African rhinos are usually gray in color, so no one knows how they came to be called black or white. The white rhino's name may come from a Dutch word that means "wide," since it has a wide, square upper lip. The white rhino grazes on grass, ripping off clumps with its powerful lips. In contrast, the black rhino (shown here) has a narrow, pointed upper lip that enables it to pluck leaves and stems from bushes and trees.

Rhinos have a keen sense of smell, but do not see well. With their great size and sharp horns, rhinos are powerful enough to overturn a car. However, they can't defend themselves against illegal hunting or against the destruction of the wild habitat they need to live. Only people can take steps that will allow the rhinoceros to remain living free in the wild.

Robin (**rahb**-in) Robins are known for their cheerful songs. In fact, male robins seem to be singing *Cheerily, Cheerily, Cheerily* as they try to attract a mate and defend a territory against other males. Robins are closely related to bluebirds, wood thrushes, and hermit thrushes—all known for their musical calls.

Sometimes a robin is called a "robin redbreast" because the chest feathers of the male robin (shown here) are reddish brown. The color of a robin's eggs is also well known, so people sometimes ask to have something painted "robin's egg" blue.

The eggs are laid in a nest that is usually built in a tree by the female robin. She gathers mud, a beakful at a time, and makes a cup-shaped foundation. She lines it with fine soft grass, on which she lays her eggs. She sits on the eggs for about two weeks, until they hatch. Then, both the mother and father bird share in bringing food to their chicks. Robins eat all sorts of food, including berries, caterpillars, and spiders, but are best known for catching worms. You may have seen a robin hopping on a lawn. It stops now and then, tips its head to one side, and sometimes grabs an earthworm and pulls it from the soil. People once thought that a robin tilts its head to one side to listen for the sound of a worm near the surface. However, a robin sees best to either side, not straight ahead, so by tilting its head, it can spot a worm or other animal hidden in the grass.

Salamander

(**sal**-uh-man-duhr) Quiet, small, and usually hidden in the daytime, salamanders are seldom noticed by people. You may find them resting under stones or within crevices of logs. The California slender salamander (shown here) is sometimes found in burrows dug by earthworms. Land salamanders hide in damp places because they need to keep their skin moist. If a salamander's skin dries out, it may die from lack of oxygen, since it does most of its breathing through its thin skin.

The lives of land salamanders are tied to water because they are amphibians—animals that usually spend part of their lives on land and part in water. In the spring, most land salamanders walk to ponds, where they mate, and where the females lay eggs. The tiny salamanders that hatch from the eggs live and grow in water until they are ready to begin life on land.

Some salamanders spend all of their lives in the water. One species, called the mud puppy, grows to be about 18 inches (46 centimeters) long. Another big North American salamander is called the hellbender. It can grow to be 30 inches (76 centimeters) long. Big or little, many salamanders have the remarkable ability to replace missing body parts. A new tail or leg can grow in a few weeks.

Salmon

(**sam**-uhn) Salmon are a favorite food fish of many people. They spend part of their lives in the northern Atlantic or Pacific Ocean, and part in freshwater streams. The Atlantic salmon relies on rivers in New England. Rivers in the Pacific Northwest, including Alaska, are vital for several salmon species. They include pink, sockeye, coho, and chinook salmon. The chinook salmon (shown here) are the biggest, with a record weight of 126 pounds (57 kilograms).

A female salmon hollows out nests in a streambed by slapping her tail in gravel. She releases thousands of eggs that are fertilized by male salmon. Tiny fish hatch from the eggs. Some kinds of young salmon spend several years in freshwater streams. Other kinds spend only a few months. Sooner or later, the young salmon head downstream to the ocean. They swim far out in the sea, catching food, growing, for a year or more. Then, they gather at the mouths of rivers that lead to the streams in which their lives started. They swim upstream, following a chemical smell to the right place. If they can reach it, the salmon mate and produce a new generation. Sadly, many dams now keep salmon from swimming far up rivers and reproducing. To help salmon survive, some dams may have to be torn down.

Sand Dollar

(**sand** dahl-uhr) When you see a sand dollar on a beach, or for sale in a seaside souvenir shop, it looks more like a round stone than the remains of a once-living animal. However, parts of the white flat disk are hollow, and it was once the outer skeleton of an animal related to sea urchins and sea stars. A live sand dollar usually lies partly buried in a sandy seabed. It is covered with short, movable spines. On its underside, the spines enable the sand dollar to creep along. They also push bits of food into its mouth—the round hole in the center of a sand dollar's shell. The food is chewed by five tiny teeth that lie inside its mouth.

Scorpion

(**skor**-pee-uhn) When darkness falls in deserts, scorpions emerge from their hideouts and begin to hunt. Scorpions also live in jungles, grasslands, and on mountains. There are more than 1,500 kinds of scorpions on Earth, and they live in a variety of habitats. Each scorpion has front claws for catching and holding insects and other prey. It also has a stinger at the tip of its tail. Venom from the stinger paralyzes an animal so the scorpion can eat it. Scorpions sting only to get food or to defend themselves. Most scorpions have venom that is no more painful than a bee sting to humans, but a few species carry deadly poison. They live mostly in tropical countries. Each year, they kill more than three thousand people.

Sea Anemone

(see uh-**nem**-uh-nee) Anemones look like beautiful flowers on the seafloor or on a coral reef. They range in size from ½ inch (1 centimeter) to about 3 feet (0.9 meter) across. They stay in one spot and capture food that swims near or drifts by on a current. Anemones are soft-bodied animals that have a mouth surrounded by tentacles. The tentacles pull in when danger threatens, and are

extended into the water when anemones feed. Stinging cells on the tentacles shoot poison into fish or other prey that touches them. Then, other cells on the tentacles shoot out threads that entangle the fish so it cannot swim away.

Nevertheless, some kinds of butterfly fish bite off pieces of anemones. Sometimes these fish are chased off by clown fish, which live near anemones. To clown fish, an anemone is a safe refuge if a predator approaches. Clown fish are protected from anemone stings by a coating of mucus on their scales.

One unusual anemone does move around the seabed because it attaches itself to a hermit crab's shell. It goes wherever the crab goes. Furthermore, when the crab abandons one shell and moves into a larger one, it grabs the anemone with its claws and sets it down on the surface of the new shell. This helps hide the crab from predators.

Sea Horse

(**see** hors) The sea horse is an unusual fish, with a head like a horse, a snout like an anteater, and a tail like a dragon. The sea horse also swims upright, with the top of its head pointed at the surface. Even more unusual is the way the sea horse reproduces. When sea horses mate, the female puts her eggs in a sac, called the brood pouch, on the male's belly. The opening in the pouch then closes for about twelve days. Baby sea horses develop inside, nourished by food within the eggs. When their father's pouch opens, about two dozen of these tiny fishes swim out. The very next day the parents mate again. A male sea horse can give birth to more than three hundred young in its breeding season, which is about seven months long.

Sea horses have small fins and swim slowly. They can't chase down animals to eat, or flee from predators. Instead, they wrap their tails around a strand of seaweed or piece of coral and wait for a small shrimp or other creature to swim by. Then, they suck the prey into their snouts. Sea horses are able to change color to match their surroundings. This helps them to ambush prey, and also to avoid being eaten themselves. About thirty-five different species of sea horses live along seacoasts all over the world. Some are only ½ inch (1.25 centimeters) long when fully grown. The biggest species, at 14 inches (35 centimeters) long, is the Pacific sea horse, which lives along the Pacific Ocean coast of North and South America.

Sea Lion

(see lie-uhn) In 1741, explorer Georg Steller discovered giant marine mammals along the northwest coast of North America. The males had shaggy manes and roared like lions, so Steller called them sea lions. These Steller, or northern, sea lions are the biggest of five kinds of sea lions that live on Earth today. Some males, or bulls, measure 11 feet (3.4 meters) long and weigh as much as ten men.

Another, smaller, sea lion lives farther south, along the western coast of the United States. The California sea lion (shown here) is intelligent and playful, and has a fine sense of balance. In the wild, it body-surfs on waves and sometimes tosses and catches fish and other objects. This sea lion is well-suited to be a performer, leaping through hoops or balancing a ball on its nose. The California sea lion is often the star of the show at zoos and aquariums.

Sea lions are swift, graceful swimmers. They steer with their hind flippers and row with their front flippers. They can dive 1,200 feet (365.8 meters) beneath the surface and stay underwater for twenty minutes before rising to take a breath. They see well in dim light, and their whiskers are very sensitive to touch. So, deep in dark water, they are still able to find and catch fish, squid, and other animals.

Sea lions go ashore to mate, and females give birth to pups there. They gather in the same places, called rookeries, year after year. A sea lion rookery is a noisy place, with bull sea lions barking, and mothers and pups calling to one another.

Sea Star

(**see** stahr) Sea stars creep along in seawater all over Earth, from tropical coral reefs to the icy ocean floor off Antarctica. You can see them washed ashore on sunny beaches or resting in tide pools. Far offshore, other sea stars live in the dark ocean depths, 3,000 feet (914.4 meters) or more below the surface. There are more than 3,600 species of sea stars, which are also called starfish. Sea stars are not fish; they are related to sand dollars and sea urchins.

Most sea stars have five arms, or rays, though some have as many as twenty. Some sea stars have short, fat rays; some have long, thin ones. On the underside of each ray are hundreds of short tentacles called tube feet. A sea star's mouth is in the center of its body, also on the underside, so it has to crawl on top of its food to eat. Sea stars are scavengers, and will eat the remains of a crab or other dead animal. When they find a clam, however, they try to get to the live animal inside its shell. A sea star tugs with its tube feet on the two halves of the clamshell, trying to pull them apart. The clam resists, but usually loses this battle. The sea star sticks its whole stomach into the partly opened shells and digests the clam. Then it pulls its stomach back into its body. Besides having this unusual way of eating, sea stars are also remarkable because they can grow new parts. A single ray can grow into a whole new sea star. The photo above shows a full-grown rainbow sea star and a little one that is in the process of growing from a broken piece.

Seal

(**seel**) All seals are slow and clumsy on land, and fast and graceful in water. Seals are so comfortable in the water that they sometimes sleep there. A layer of fat called **blubber** helps protect them from cold. At times, though, they drag themselves out of the water and rest on shore or on a big rock. They sleep in the warmth of the sun before plunging back into the water to hunt. Seals also come ashore in safe gathering places called rookeries, where they mate and females give birth to their pups.

A harbor seal (shown here) steers with its front flippers and pushes itself through the water with its rear flippers. It is one kind of a group called the earless seals. These seals have little ear openings on the sides of their heads, but no outer flaps of skin. They are related to another group of marine mammals that do have little ear flaps. This group includes fur seals and sea lions. They use their flippers in the opposite way from the earless seals—they swim with their front flippers and steer with the rear ones.

The most unusual of all seal relatives is an arctic mammal called the walrus. A male walrus may weigh more than 1 ton (0.9 tonne). With its long tusks, it digs clams from the sea bottom.

Shark

(shahrk) A shark does not have a single bone in its body. Its skeleton is made of a tough material called cartilage. (You can feel cartilage in your own nose and ears.) There are nearly four hundred kinds of sharks on Earth. Some have bodies shaped like the blue shark (shown here), but sharks come in many different shapes. Angel sharks have flat bodies, like fish called flounder. One group of unusual-looking sharks is the hammerheads. They have broad, flat heads shaped like a double-headed hammer. Their eyes look out from the tips of the "hammers."

Most species of sharks have many, many sharp teeth, but the teeth of the horn shark are flat on top. They crush the shells of crabs they catch. On rare occasions, a few kinds of sharp-toothed sharks bite people. They include mako, bull, tiger, and great white sharks. Each year, millions of people swim where sharks live, but only about one hundred are bitten—usually because a shark mistakes a person for a seal or other food it likes. The biggest sharks are harmless to people. Basking sharks and whale sharks swim with their huge mouths open, gulping down tiny animals and plants that they filter from the water.

Sheep

(**sheep**) Sheep are among the most useful of all animals raised by people. Younger sheep produce meat called lamb; older sheep produce meat called mutton. Sheepskin can be made into a soft leather used to make fine gloves. Sheepskin with the hair left on is made into warm hats, coats, and bedspreads. Living sheep produce something else of great value: their hair, which is called wool. Their long coats of wool are usually cut off, or sheared, in the late spring or early summer. Being sheared is like getting a very short haircut. A sheep's hair grows in again before cold autumn weather arrives.

Some breeds of sheep have long, straight hair that is good for making carpets. One variety of sheep, the merino, has a dense coat of fine, kinky hair, and its wool is ideal for making soft sweaters. The color of wool varies from one variety of sheep to another, but all wool can be made into warm and durable clothing.

A male sheep is called a ram, while a female is a ewe, pronounced "yoo." In the spring, ewes give birth to one or two lambs, which can stand and walk soon after being born. Lambs nurse milk from their mother. Both a ewe and her lamb learn to recognize the other's voice and scent so they can find each other in a large flock of sheep, which may number in the thousands on some ranches. Lambs are playful. They run and leap, alone or with others. Lambs sometimes play "king of the hill" on a hay bale or other high place.

Shrimp

(**shrimp**) Shrimp are related to lobsters and crayfish. They are crustaceans, with hard outer skeletons that must be shed and replaced with roomier ones as they grow. A shrimp does this eight times before reaching its full size. For most shrimp, "full size" isn't very big. Many species measure just 1 inch (2.5 centimeters) long or less. Mantis shrimps can grow to 12 inches (30 centimeters) long. Big or little, shrimp are important animals in the ocean, partly because they are eaten by so many creatures. Also, some shrimp clean the faces and bodies of eels and other fish. Coral reefs are the homes of many colorful shrimp, including this candy stripe shrimp (shown here).

Skunk

(**skuhngk**) The striped skunk (shown here) is the most common skunk in North America. It is about the size of a house cat. Each night it hunts for food, digging into the soil with sharp claws to catch earthworms and grubs. It also eats grasshoppers, mice, and berries. If a person or dog gets too close to a striped skunk, it usually defends itself by first stamping its front feet and hissing. Then it turns its rear end toward the intruder and raises its bushy tail straight into the air. If these warnings do not work, the skunk sprays a smelly fluid from two glands beneath its tail. The scent of skunk spray can be smelled more than 1 mile (1.6 kilometers) away, and lingers on objects for many days. The striped skunk has a smaller relative, the spotted skunk, that does handstands. It walks on its front feet, sometimes in play and sometimes as a warning that it is about to spray its powerful scent.

Sloth (**slawth**) or (**slahth**)

A person who is not active is sometimes called a "couch potato." Long ago, such a lazy person was often called a "sloth." This name was also given to two closely related animals that live in the rain forests of Central and South America: the two-toed sloth and the three-toed sloth. The three-toed sloth (shown here) is slightly smaller than the two-toed sloth, which is about 2 feet (0.6 meter) long.

Sloths are not lazy; they simply do not need to move fast or far during their entire lives. Sloths seldom come down from trees. They eat, sleep, mate, and have young while holding onto tree trunks and limbs with their long, curved claws. A baby sloth clings to its mother and nurses milk from her until it is ready to clamber about among the trees and vines of its tropical forest home.

Sloths spend much of their lives hanging upside down beneath branches. They travel that way, too, one slow step at a time, then stop to eat leaves, buds, and twigs. The three-toed sloth is especially fond of the giant leaves of the cecropia tree. Sloths are not often seen by eagles and other predators because they stay still so much, and because tiny green plants called algae grow on their brownish-gray fur. The algae's green color helps sloths blend into their leafy surroundings.

Slug

(**sluhg**) Slugs are close relatives of snails, but have no shells. Like snails, they creep along on a muscular foot. Shiny, slippery slime oozes from the slug's foot, making travel easier. The slime is sticky, so a slug can climb straight up a post or even cling upside down. Slugs need to keep their skin moist. Since they are not protected by a shell, slugs are usually found in damp places. They come out at night or on rainy days. A slug can scrunch its soft body into a lump or stretch into a long, narrow shape. Most land slugs have dull colors and match the earth and leaves on the ground where they live, but some slugs in northern California are yellow-green. They are often about 6 inches (15 centimeters) long, so they are called banana slugs. Students at the University of California at Santa Cruz chose Banana Slugs as the name of their athletic teams.

Snail

(**snayl**) Snails can be found in freshwater, in seawater, and on land. They are mollusks, related to clams, octopuses, and their closest relatives, slugs. Both slugs and snails are known to move slowly. That's why traffic reporters sometimes say that cars are moving at a snail's pace. A snail carries its shell as it moves. If it senses danger, it pulls its whole body inside the shell. When danger is past, the snail soon extends its tentacles. Both land snails (shown here) and slugs have four tentacles on the front of their head that help them sense their surroundings. The long tentacles have simple eyes at their tips that sense light and shadow.

Snake

(**snayk**) Snakes are colorful, fascinating, and mostly harmless **reptiles** that live on every continent except Antarctica. Among nearly three thousand species of snakes, there is a great variety of size, color, and behavior. The smallest snake is a 4-inch-(10 centimeter) long blind snake of the tropics. The largest is the anaconda, which can grow to be 35 feet (10.7 meters)—as long as a school bus. There are sea snakes that dive 160 feet (48.8 meters) down in the ocean, and the paradise tree snake of Asia that glides through the air from tree to tree.

Well-known poisonous snakes include rattlesnakes, cobras, mambas, and copperheads. The great majority of snakes, including racers, garter snakes, and the mountain king snake (shown here) are harmless to people. They are useful to humans because they kill mice and other pests. Most snakes see well, but have no external ears. They do not hear, but can detect vibrations caused by moving creatures. A snake's most powerful sense involves its forked tongue. The tongue picks up scent **molecules** from the air, then brings them to a special scent organ in the roof of the snake's mouth. Many people expect snakes to be slimy, but discover they are dry, smooth, and pleasant to touch.

Spider

(**spide**-uhr) Some spiders are so "itsy-bitsy" that they are not much bigger than the period at the end of this sentence. Those called tarantulas can measure 10 inches (25 centimeters) across their bodies and legs. Big or little, every spider has eight legs and a pair of fangs that inject poison. However, of more than thirty-four thousand kinds of spiders on Earth, only a few are dangerous to humans. The small black widow (shown here) has a strong poison that can cause death. Most spiders have **venom** that is too weak to affect people, or their fangs cannot even pierce human skin, but the venom is strong enough to kill insects for food. In its lifetime, a spider may eat hundreds of insects, including many that are pests to people.

Most spiders have eight eyes. The spiders with the keenest vision are predators that ambush their prey, leap on it, or chase it. They include wolf, crab, and jumping spiders. Some spiders spin webs made of silk that flows from glands within their abdomens. Webs can be shaped like funnels, domes, or wagon wheels. Some webs have sticky lines that can trap a moth or other insects. Then, the spider rushes to the insect, bites it, and wraps it in silk, saving it to eat later.

Squid

(**skwid**) Squids are among the most common and important animals of the world's oceans. There are 375 species that range in size from 1 inch (2.5 centimeters) to 70 feet (21.3 meters) long. Parts of some deep-ocean squids glow in the dark. All squids have big eyes, but the giant

squid has the largest eyes of any animal on Earth—the size of dinner plates. It spends most of its life in the dark depths of the ocean, more than 1 mile (2 kilometers) below the surface.

Squids, related to octopuses, have eight arms and two long tentacles. Grabbing a fish or other animal with the suckers on its tentacles, a squid brings it to the hard, sharp beak in its mouth. While it eats, the squid itself may be in danger of being eaten. Squids are a favorite food of seals, sharks, penguins, and whales. They are sometimes attacked when they gather in huge numbers to mate (shown here). Hundreds of squid beaks were once found in the stomach of a sperm whale.

Whether hunting or being hunted, a squid moves swiftly through the water. It relaxes its muscles and inhales water. Then it tightens its muscles and the water spurts out behind, pushing the squid forward. Quickly taking water in and squirting it out, again and again, the squid jets through the water.

Squirrel

(**skwuhrl**) The red squirrel (shown here), also called the chickaree, is one of five species of tree squirrels in North America. It lives mostly in mountain ranges or northern areas where spruces, firs, and other evergreen trees grow. Red squirrels store food for winter by making piles of seed-bearing evergreen cones. Gray squirrels, a familiar sight in many suburbs and city parks, store food by digging small holes in the soil and burying an acorn, walnut, or other tree seed in each one. High overhead, gray squir-

rels are surefooted travelers, able to leap from tree to tree and even walk along telephone wires. They often outwit people who try to keep them from reaching sunflower seeds put in bird feeders. Tree squirrels are related to ground squirrels that live in western North America. Ground squirrels store their winter seed supply in underground burrows they dig.

Stingray

(**sting**-ray) Just like sharks, stingrays do not have a single bone in their bodies. A stingray's skeleton is made of cartilage —the same strong but flexible material that is in your nose and ears. Manta rays, skates, and sharks also have cartilage skeletons, and are related to stingrays.

All over the world, there are more than one hundred kinds of rays. The biggest (shown here) measure 6 feet (1.8 meters) across. Big or little, all rays

have flattened bodies and broad, winglike fins. When they flap their fins, they look like graceful birds flying underwater. Rays usually stay on the seabed, where they eat clams and other shelled animals. Stingrays are named for a poisonous spine at the base of their tails. This spine can give a painful wound to someone who accidentally steps on a hidden stingray.

Stork

(**stork**) Storks are water birds, with long legs for wading in shallow water, and long necks and bills for reaching underwater to catch fish and other prey. The saddle-billed stork of Africa (shown here) is one of seventeen kinds of stork on Earth. The world's best-known species is the white stork of Europe. It is often pictured on birth announcements because of the myth that newborn babies are delivered by storks. White storks build large nests on rooftops in European cities. In late summer, they begin a remarkable migration, flying 6,000 miles (9,600 kilometers) or more to wintering grounds in Africa. In the spring, they fly all the way back, returning to their same nests in Europe. Storks are strong fliers, but also smart fliers. Like hawks, vultures, and many other birds, they take advantage of rising warm air and can travel long distances without using much energy.

For many years, it was thought that no storks lived in North America. Then, scientists learned that a bird named the wood ibis was actually a stork. This large black-and-white wading bird is now called the wood stork. It does not migrate. Sadly, only a few thousand wood storks survive in the southeastern United States.

Swan

(**swahn**) There are few sights in nature as beautiful as a white swan swimming gracefully in the dark waters of a pond. Swans are big waterbirds, related to geese and ducks. Of the eight species of swans on Earth, six are white, but one in Australia is black and another in South America has a black neck and white body.

In North America, there are three kinds of swans: the tundra, the trumpeter, and the mute. The mute swan (shown here), brought to North America from England, has an orange beak, while the other two have black beaks. Tundra and trumpeter swans make loud calls but mute swans can only make a grunting sound to call their young and a hissing sound to threaten enemies. Swans hiss at people who come too close to their nest or young, which are called cygnets. When cygnets are small, they sometimes ride on the back of a parent swan.

Swans cannot dive, so they dip their heads and long necks underwater to eat water plants, insects, and other small animals. To take flight, a swan beats its wings rapidly while running along the water's surface. Once in the air, a swan can fly 40 miles (64 kilometers) an hour. Mute swans do not migrate, but trumpeter and tundra swans do. Some tundra swans fly more than 2,000 miles (3,219 kilometers), from Canada to North Carolina.

Termite

(**tuhr**-mite) Underground, or inside a log or the floorboards of a house, live some of the most abundant insects on Earth —termites. They live in colonies, sometimes numbering in the hundreds, sometimes in the millions. A termite colony has one queen, one king, and many soldiers and workers. The workers (shown here) get food, take care of eggs and young, and feed the king and queen. The queen, by far the biggest termite in a colony, may lay thousands of eggs in a single day.

Soldier termites guard the colony. Some have massive heads and jaws. They can't feed themselves, so workers give them food. Many kinds of termites eat only wood. They could not exist without microscopic, one-celled organisms called protozoa that live in their gut. The protozoa enable the termites to digest their meals of wood. When their wooden meals come from houses, barns, and other structures built by humans, termites can cause a lot of damage. In the United States, wood-eating termites usually have an underground nest, and the workers build slender tubes of soil on a house's foundation so they can reach its wooden boards. In Africa, termite workers cement bits of earth together with their saliva and make large mounds or slender columns up to 20 feet (6.1 meters) tall. The tough walls of these structures usually protect the termite nest within.

Tiger

(**tie**-guhr) The tiger is Earth's biggest cat. It is also one of the most admired and feared of all animals. A tiger's roar can be heard from a distance of at least 2 miles (3.2 kilometers). In parts of India, the roar of a Bengal tiger causes people to shiver with fear, because the tiger is one of the few animals on Earth that actually hunts humans.

Most tigers avoid people. With patience, on soft pads on the bottoms of their feet, they quietly creep up on deer, wild pigs, buffalo, and even monkeys. A tiger usually kills its prey by gripping its neck, breaking its backbone, or cutting off its air supply. Even though tigers are great hunters, they may stalk a dozen animals before they are able to catch one.

Long ago, millions of tigers lived all over Asia, from snowy Siberia to the jungles of Burma. Now only a few thousand remain. Tigers are still being killed and their wild forest habitat is being destroyed. About two hundred Siberian tigers survive in the wild. The Siberian is the biggest of all tigers. Males can grow to weigh 750 pounds (340 kilograms) and measure 13 feet (4 meters) long. Four other varieties of tigers live in parts of China, India, and Thailand. In places where the weather is hot, tigers often cool off in rivers and ponds. Unlike most cats, they enjoy swimming and playing in water.

Toad

(**tohd**) One of spring's sweetest sounds is not the song of a bird. It is the trill of a toad. As the weather and the water warm in the spring, toads gather in ponds, swamps, and other wetlands. The males push air from their lungs into a throat sac that swells like a bubblegum bubble. They release the air and make a long, trilling song. It is mating time, and the males are competing for the attention of female toads. After mating, strings of fertilized eggs are left in the water. Tiny tadpoles hatch from the eggs. They eat algae and other plants, grow bigger, and develop the legs that will enable them to hop along on land.

A toad is always welcome in a garden. It hides by day, then hunts for insects at night. When an earwig runs along the ground or a little moth flies by, the toad flicks out its sticky tongue, snags the insect, then swallows it. Toads have no teeth.

Toads have rough, bumpy skin. They look like they have warts, and people once believed that handling a toad would give a person warts. This is not true. However, a toad in danger may defend itself by giving off a stinging fluid from its skin.

Tortoise

(tort-uhs) Tortoises are a special group of turtles that live only on land. Most tortoises have high, dome-shaped shells, and thick, sturdy legs that are useful for walking, not swimming. To defend itself, a tortoise pulls its head as far as possible into its shell and forms a shield with its scaly front legs.

Many tortoises live in deserts, and dig burrows that provide relief from the searing heat. The tunnels dug by a desert tortoise of North America (shown here) can be used by several tortoises at once. Gopher tortoises of the southern United States also dig burrows up to 30 feet (9.1 meters) long. However, some tortoises are just too big to dig a burrow. The giant land tortoise of the Galápagos Islands, east of Ecuador, can weigh more than 600 pounds (272 kilograms). The islands were named for their tortoises by Spanish explorers. In Spanish, *galápago* means tortoise.

All tortoises are slow-moving plant eaters. Galápagos tortoises do not begin to feed until the sun has warmed their huge bodies. They eat a variety of leaves and berries, and even the juicy but spiny pads of the prickly pear cactus. The cactus pads provide both food and water, which is usually scarce on the Galápagos Islands.

Toucan (**too**-kan)

The bill of a toucan is almost as long as its body. It makes the bird look bigger than it really is, and may discourage attacks by predators. Having this kind of bill also helps toucans get food. With its long bill, a toucan can perch on a sturdy tree limb, yet reach berries or nuts from a branch tip. A toucan often picks a berry with the tip of its beak, then tosses its head back so the berry drops down its throat. Toucan bills look heavy, but are lightweight, and strong enough to crack nutshells. Toucans also eat spiders, lizards, and insects they find high in the trees of Central and South American rain forests. They also use their bills to pick away pieces of wood to enlarge a hole in a tree, making a hollow space big enough to lay eggs and raise young.

Toucans are among the most colorful birds of the tropics. The keel-billed toucan has a bright yellow chest and five colors on its beak. The toco toucan (shown here) has a bill of three colors, and also has a circle of blue skin around each eye.

Colorful toucans flash through the jungle in groups. They fly and feed together, and even play games of catch, tossing berries back and forth. They also have a lot to say to one another, including chirps, yelps, croaks, barks, and rattles. Visitors to rain forests usually hear toucans calling high overhead from dawn to dusk. Toucans remind us that rain forests are full of life and wonder. They remind us that these forests must be saved.

Trout

(**trout**) Lake trout live in the deep water of big lakes. However, to a person who fishes, the word *trout* usually brings to mind a cool, clean, swift-flowing stream. Several kinds of trout, including the brook trout and rainbow trout (shown here) thrive in rivers and creeks that are not too warm or polluted.

A trout usually finds a place to rest out of the main current. It often waits in a quiet pool just below a waterfall, or downstream of a rock. It faces upstream and waits for an insect to drift near, then gulps it down. On some spring days, mayflies rise to the water's surface and then begin to flutter away. *Splash!* The beautiful colors of a trout flash in the sun as it leaps out of the water to catch the flying insect.

Tuna

(**too**-nuh) Tuna are among the fastest of all fish. They swim the open seas, eating their way through schools of herring, anchovies, and mackerel. Tuna are sometimes called tunny. Fish called bonita, albacore, and skipjacks are all varieties of tuna.

Bluefin tuna (shown here) live in the Atlantic Ocean. A bluefin can live at least thirty years and grow to be longer than 10 feet (3 meters). It can zoom through the water at 20 miles (32 kilometers) an hour. The shape of its body and fins allows the bluefin tuna to move swiftly. Since it is a big, active fish, it needs more oxygen than many other kinds of fish. Organs called gills take oxygen from the water. The gills of bluefin tuna are ten times larger than those of other kinds of fish of the same size.

Turkey

(**tuhr**-kee) According to historians, the turkey was given its name because Europeans once believed that this bird came from the country called Turkey. Today, everyone knows that the turkey is a native of North America. Wild turkeys were nearly wiped out by hunters, but now more than one million live in the United States, Canada, and Mexico. Wild turkeys roam in woods and fields, eating insects, worms, and seeds. They are especially fond of acorns from oak trees. At night, they fly up into trees and roost on branches, safe from predators that might catch them on the ground.

Wild turkeys are the ancestors of turkeys that are raised on farms and killed to provide meat for people, especially at Thanksgiving time. These domestic turkeys, usually white in color, are quite different from wild turkeys. They are plump, with large chest muscles that provide people with breast meat. They have wings, but are too heavy to fly. Wild turkeys are strong flyers, and can run 25 miles (40 kilometers) an hour. They are slim except at mating time in late winter and early spring, when the males, called toms, puff out their feathers and spread their tail feathers in a fan shape (shown here). The bare skin on their heads and necks turns bright red. This grand display is meant for female turkeys, called hens. Toms also try to attract hens by making a loud gobbling sound.

Turtle

(**tuhrt**-l) A turtle's shell may seem like a garage in which it parks its body, but a turtle cannot live apart from its shell. The shell is made of bone, with the turtle's ribs and backbone attached on the inside. The outside of the shell is like a coat of armor. If a raccoon or other predator attacks, a turtle pulls its head, feet, and tail tightly into its shell. The shells of box turtles give the best protection. A hinged front on the bottom half of the shell closes tightly over the box turtle's front legs and head.

Some turtles cannot hide completely inside their shells. They must defend themselves in other ways. The musk turtle gives off a bad smell that usually makes a predator leave it alone. Snapping turtles and softshelled turtles have strong jaws and sharp claws for defense. Like all turtles, the snapping turtle is toothless, but it is able to catch fish, frogs, and young ducks in its powerful jaws. The alligator snapping turtle often waits underwater with its mouth wide open. On its tongue, a piece of pink flesh wiggles like a worm. It may lure a fish close enough for the turtle to catch it and gulp it down. An alligator snapper can weigh as much as 300 pounds (136 kilograms). It is the largest turtle that lives in freshwater, but the biggest turtles of all live in the ocean. The leatherback sea turtle can weigh as much as 1 ton (0.9 tonne).

Vulture

(**vuhl**-chuhr) On the ground, vultures may not seem very appealing. They are **scavengers** that feed on the carcasses of dead animals. Some people think this is disgusting. However, other predators, such as lions, raccoons, and eagles also eat the remains of animals they did not kill. In Africa, vultures are often chased from an animal carcass by lions or other predators. Nothing goes to waste in nature, and vultures are very good at finding and cleaning up animals that have been killed by cars, disease, or other animals. By getting rid of decaying carcasses, vultures may prevent the spread of some diseases.

Once a vulture spreads its wings and rises into the sky, it becomes a bird of graceful flight. It can sail on rising air currents for many minutes without flapping its wings. The vulture scans the land below, searching with its sharp eyesight for an animal carcass. One species, the turkey vulture, has an unusually good sense of smell. It flies closer to the ground than other vultures because odors in the air can guide it to a decaying carcass.

The black vulture (shown here) and the turkey vulture are the two most common kinds of vultures in North America. In all, there are twenty-two species of vultures on Earth, including those called condors, which are among the world's largest flying birds.

Wasp

(wahsp) Imagine trying to build yourself a home from stuff you put in your mouth and chew. That's what wasps do. Worker wasps bite off wood fibers from fence posts, wood piles, and tree bark. They chew the fibers into a moist pulp, then use this material to make walls and other parts of their nest (shown here). As they work, they sometimes

bend their bodies sharply at the waist. Unlike most insects, wasps have a slender waist between the upper part of their body—the head and thorax—and their abdomen.

The most vital parts of a wasp nest are little rooms, called cells, in which the wasp queen lays eggs. Larvae hatch from the eggs. In order to develop into adults, the larvae must be fed some sort of animal food. Worker wasps go hunting. They come back with caterpillars and other insects, and feed bits of this food to the wasp larvae. By the end of summer, a wasp colony may include hundreds of workers, which are all females. Most wasps die in the fall. Some queens hide and rest in the winter, ready to start new colonies in the spring. Old wasp nests are never used again, so a queen wasp's first job is to begin work on a brand-new nest.

Some wasp nests are built in plain sight; for example, under the eaves of a house. Some are built underground. Wasps called yellow jackets usually build their nests in a hollow space in the soil. If someone accidentally steps too close to a yellow jacket nest, worker wasps try to defend their colony by stinging the intruder.

Whale

(**hwayl**) Some dinosaurs were huge, but today, there are even bigger animals alive on Earth: whales. The blue whale is the largest animal that ever lived. A male blue whale can grow to be 100 feet (30.5 meters) long, and weigh 160 tons (145 tonnes). That is more weight than forty of the world's heaviest elephants!

Whales are mammals, not fish. Although a sperm whale hunting for squid may dive 5,000 feet (1,524 meters) below the surface, it must come up for a breath of air. A sperm whale breathes through an opening at the top of its head called a blowhole. Sperm whales, beluga whales, killer whales, and smaller whales called dolphins all have one blowhole and teeth for catching the food they eat.

A second group of whales has two blowholes and no teeth. These whales have food-catchers that look like giant combs or curtains, called baleen plates, that hang from the roofs of their mouths. This group of whales is called baleen whales. They engulf great mouthfuls of seawater. Shrimp, small fish, and other tiny creatures are trapped by the baleen, then swallowed. Baleen whales include the blue whale, gray whale, and humpback whale. A humpback (shown here) is lunging out of the water, or breaching. Whale numbers are much lower than they once were because so many were killed for their meat; their fat, called blubber; and other parts useful to humans.

Wolf

(**wulf**) The howl of the wolf is one of the most exciting sounds in all of nature. Wolves live in large areas of wild land away from people and are a symbol of this wilderness. People once feared wolves, which reportedly killed some humans in Europe long ago. However, scientists say that no healthy wild wolf has ever killed a person in North America. While people have no reason to fear wolves, wolves have every reason to fear people. So many wolves were killed that they were wiped out in nearly all parts of the United States. Given protection, wolves have returned to some wild areas in the West. Wolves caught in Canada were released in Yellowstone National Park, and are thriving there.

Wolves live in family groups called packs. A pack often travels dozens of miles (kilometers) a day while hunting deer, moose, elk, or other prey. Each pack has a large territory in which it lives, and howling is one way it defends its territory. Wolves also mark the borders of their territory by leaving scent marks of urine, just as dogs do. Wolves are the ancestors of dogs, and have the same qualities that people like in dogs. Although wolves do not make good pets, they are intelligent and playful. All of the members of a pack care for young wolves, called cubs. Once people learn what wolves are really like, they will admire and respect this large, wild member of the dog family.

Woodpecker (**wud**-pek-uhr)

The season of spring is announced by the beautiful melodies of robins and cardinals—and by the loud hammering and drumming sounds of woodpeckers. Male woodpeckers beat their strong beaks on hollow trees and sometimes on metal roofs. They make loud sounds to attract a mate, and to defend their territory from other males. After mating, male woodpeckers chip out a nesting hole in a tree. And in all seasons woodpeckers peck at trees to reach ants and other insects hidden under bark and inside the wood. They catch insects with a long, sticky tongue.

Woodpeckers live almost everywhere there are trees. Over two hundred species exist worldwide. In the American Southwest, gila woodpeckers usually make nest holes in tall cactus plants instead of trees.

Worm (**wuhrm**)

There are many kinds of worms, including tapeworms and flatworms, but when most people hear the word *worm* they picture an earthworm (shown here). There are many kinds of earthworms, too. They include worms in Australia that are sometimes 12 feet (3.7 meters) long. Most earthworms are just a few inches (centimeters) long when they stretch out long and thin. Earthworms can also squeeze their segments together and become short and fat.

Earthworms are most active at night. In fact, one common North American earthworm is called the night crawler. Worms eat dead leaves. They mix and move soil. Their burrows allow air and water to flow down into the soil. Quiet, crawling earthworms are good for the soil and the plants that grow in it.

Zebra

(**zee**-bruh) A herd of zebras racing across a dusty grassland in eastern Africa is one of the most exciting of all sights in nature. The plains zebra (shown here) is the most common of several kinds. Zebras are related to horses and donkeys. They look like horses with black-and-white stripes, and in many ways they behave as horses do, too.

One male zebra, a stallion, leads a family group made up of several females, or mares, and their young. The young stay with their mothers for several years. A newborn zebra, called a foal, is able to stand and walk within a few minutes of its birth. This is important for its survival. Zebras are always on the move, seeking grass to eat and water to drink. They are also hunted by lions and hyenas.

Every zebra is covered with black-and-white stripes, but the pattern of stripes varies from one animal to the next. This may help zebras recognize one another. Sometimes one zebra gives another member of its family group friendly nibbles on its back and neck. Zebras also stand in pairs and rest their heads on one another's backs. Facing in different directions, the two zebras watch out for predators.

Glossary

Page numbers indicate first use of glossary terms.

amphibians, 43, animals that usually spend part of their life cycle on land but must lay their eggs in water. Amphibians include frogs, toads, and salamanders.

bioluminescence, 41, light emitted by living things, such as the light given off by fireflies.

bivalves, 26, animals in the mollusk group that are surrounded and protected by two outer shells that are hinged on one side. Bivalves include clams, oysters, and mussels.

blubber, 98, a thick layer of fat that keeps dolphins and whales from losing too much body heat to the cold waters around them.

canopy, 73, the topmost layer of a forest, made of the branches and leaves of the tallest trees. Some birds, insects, and other creatures live only in the canopy.

chrysalis, 15, the shell-like covering of the pupa stage of a butterfly's life cycle. The adult butterfly emerges from the chrysalis.

clans, 56, groups of hyenas, led by adult females, that also include males and young. Each clan defends a home range or territory against other hyena clans.

cocoon, 69, a silky covering of the pupa stage of a moth's life cycle. The adult moth emerges from the cocoon.

colonies, 7, groups of insects that live together, with different individuals having different jobs, such as getting food or defending the colony. Honeybees, termites, and ants live in colonies.

crustaceans, 10, animals with a hard outer skeleton, two pairs of antennae, biting jaws, and five pairs of jointed legs. Crustaceans include crayfish, lobsters, crabs, and copepods.

extinction, 77, the process by which all members of a species die, and the species no longer exists.

food chains, 84, series of living things that are linked by their food relationships, in which one living thing eats another. For example, plant seeds are eaten by a mouse, which is eaten by an owl.

habitat, 23, the kind of local environment where a plant or an animal normally lives. For example, many lizards live in desert habitats, and cannot survive in forest habitats.

hatch, 6, to emerge from or break out of an egg.

larvae, 41, the active young stage in the development of many insects. A moth or butterfly larva is often called a caterpillar.

mammals, 10, warm-blooded animals with hair or fur. Mammals nourish their young with milk produced by the mother's body.

marsupials, 59, mammals that are born at an early stage of development and must stay attached to the mother's nipple while they develop further. The young are often sheltered in a pouch located on the mother's abdomen. Kangaroos and opossums are marsupials.

mate, 6, to come together for breeding. Male and female animals mate to produce young.

migrate, 18, to move from one area to another, then return. Many birds migrate south in the autumn and fly northward in the spring.

molecules, 104, the smallest possible amounts of a substance that still has the physical and chemical characteristics of that substance.

mollusks, 26, animals without bones, most of which are protected by a shell. They include snails and squid, and such bivalves as clams.

nocturnal, 76, active at night.

omnivores, 11, animals that commonly eat both plants and animals.

pollination, 13, the process by which flowering plants reproduce. Male pollen is carried by wind, insects, bats, or in other ways to the female parts of flowers, where fertilization takes place that results in the growth of seeds.

predator, 21, an animal that kills other animals for food.

prey, 21, animals killed by predators for food.

primate, 9, a mammal with a well-developed brain, eyes that face forward, and humanlike hands. Primates include monkeys, chimpanzees, gorillas, and humans.

reptiles, 104, animals with backbones that breathe with lungs and have an outer covering of scales or bony plates. Reptiles depend on the sun and other outside sources to warm their bodies, so they are called "cold-blooded." They include snakes, lizards, turtles, and alligators.

rodent, 12, a mammal that has a pair of long, chisel-like teeth at the front of both lower and upper jaws. The teeth are used for gnawing and cutting plant foods. Rodents include mice, rats, squirrels, beavers, and chipmunks.

savanna, 21, tall grassland with scattered trees or clumps of trees.

scavengers, 118, animals that feed on the remains of dead animals they find. Lions, foxes, eagles, and many other predators are also scavengers.

selective breeding, 34, choosing animals for mating in order to produce young with desired looks and other qualities. Selective breeding has produced cows that give more milk, as well as the great variety of dog breeds.

species, 8, a group of living things that have many characteristics in common, which make them all different from other species. Members of a species interbreed with one another but not with members of other species.

talons, 38, sharp, curved claws on the feet of owls, eagles, and other predatory birds.

territory, 30, an area defended by an animal or group of animals against others of its own species.

tundra, 18, a cold, treeless area where plant life consists of mosses, lichens, and low-growing shrubs.

venom, 105, a poisonous liquid, delivered by bite or sting, from such animals as scorpions, honeybees, and rattlesnakes.

Index

Pronunciation Guide

In the *Scholastic Encyclopedia of Animals* the pronunciation of each animal's name is shown in parentheses, as in **ostrich** (**ahs**-trich).

In writing, one letter of the alphabet may stand for different sounds. For example, the **a** in **mad** and the **a** in **make** stand for two different sounds, and so do the **s** in **say** and the **s** in **rise**. This encyclopedia uses a special alphabet to show how to pronounce the names of the animals. The list below shows the letters used for each sound in the pronunciations. In pronunciations, these letters have only one sound. The example words show you the sound each one stands for. In longer words, dark letters in the pronunciation are spoken louder than the lighter letters.

a	as in **mad** (**mad**), **bat** (**bat**)	**oh**	as in **no** (**noh**), **grow** (**groh**), **toe** (**toh**), **alone** (uh-**lohn**)
ah	as in **father** (**fah**TH-uhr), **dark** (**dahrk**), **dot** (**daht**)	**oi**	as in **soil** (**soil**), **toy** (**toi**)
air	as in **fair** (**fair**), **care** (**kair**)	**oo**	as in **pool** (**pool**), **rude** (**rood**), **music** (**myoo**-zik), **few** (**fyoo**)
aw	as in **paw** (**paw**), **tall** (**tawl**)	**or**	as in **corn** (**korn**), **more** (**mor**)
ay	as in **day** (**day**), **made** (**mayd**), **same** (**saym**)	**ou**	as in **out** (**out**), **allow** (uh-**lou**)
b	as in **bad** (**bad**), **tub** (**tuhb**)	**p**	as in **pan** (**pan**), **top** (**tahp**)
ch	as in **chin** (**chin**), **bench** (**bench**)	**r**	as in **rip** (**rip**), **pour** (**por**)
d	as in **deer** (**dir**), **red** (**red**)	**s**	as in **side** (**side**), **miss** (**mis**), **race** (**rays**), **yes** (**yes**)
e	as in **net** (**net**), **send** (**send**)	**sh**	as in **ship** (**ship**), **rush** (**ruhsh**)
ee	as in **teeth** (**teeth**), **bean** (**been**)	**t**	as in **tub** (**tuhb**), **hat** (**hat**)
f	as in **far** (**fahr**), **enough** (i-**nuhf**)	**th**	as in **thin** (**thin**), **bath** (**bath**)
g	as in **get** (**get**), **flag** (**flag**)	**TH**	as in **this** (**THis**), **breathe** (**breeTH**)
h	as in **hand** (**hand**), **ahead** (uh-**hed**)	**u**	as in **put** (**put**), **book** (**buk**)
hw	as in **white** (**hwite**), **whale** (**hwayl**)	**uh**	as in **above** (uh-**buhv**), **listen** (**lis**-uhn), **pencil** (**pen**-suhl), **lemon** (**lem**-uhn), **fun** (**fuhn**)
i	as in **big** (**big**), **sit** (**sit**), **dear** (**dir**), **here** (**hir**)	**uhr**	as in **later** (**late**-uhr), **burn** (**buhrn**), **work** (**wuhrk**)
ie, i-e	as in **lie** (**lie**), **iron** (**ie**-uhrn), **ripe** (**ripe**)	**v**	as in **very** (**ver**-ee), **five** (**five**)
j	as in **jar** (**jahr**), **edge** (**ej**)	**w**	as in **well** (**wel**), **between** (bi-**tween**)
k	as in **keep** (**keep**), **sock** (**sahk**)	**y**	as in **yes** (**yes**), **few** (**fyoo**), **music** (**myoo**-zik)
l	as in **lap** (**lap**), **tell** (**tel**), **bottle** (**baht**-l)	**z**	as in **zebra** (**zee**-bruh), **rose** (**rohz**)
m	as in **mad** (**mad**), **lamb** (**lam**)	**zh**	as in **measure** (**mezh**-uhr)
n	as in **now** (**nou**), **ten** (**ten**), **know** (**noh**), **mitten** (**mit**-n)		
ng	as in **sing** (**sing**), **single** (**sing**-guhl)